A Compendium of Medical Practitioners

Anton P. Sohn

To Jim and
Nancy
Friends for 10+
years "Andy"
Arthur P. Sohn
9.27.97

Greasewood Press / Reno

The Healers of 19th-Century
NEVADA

Greasewood Press
Pathology/350
Reno, Nev. 89557

1 2 3 4 5 6 7 8 9 10

Production of *The Healers of 19th-Century Nevada*
was made possible by a grant from
The Great Basin History of Medicine Program
of the Department of Pathology,
University of Nevada School of Medicine

Library of Congress Catalog Card Number 96-076748
ISBN 0-9649759-2-0

Text Production and Formatting by
    Anton Phillip Sohn
Jacket Design by
    Carrie Nelson House

For Owen Bolstad and Roy Hogan
Fellow Nevada Travelers

I am Indian.
There is no humiliation
Left to me,
Yet I know dignity.
There was no emancipation proclamation
For the accursed redskin,
Yet I know freedom.
Through it all, one thought
Has saved me—survival.
For survival
Is a matter of spirit
And my spirit
Remains unbroken.

—From *I am Indian*
Patricia Barry, Fort Bidwell

Contents

Acknowledgments

For most of a decade I have been researching local and national archives for Nevada's medical heritage. As a former medical officer in the United States Army, I was drawn to the military and its important history in our state. Unfortunately, virtually all of the Army surgeons who served in Nevada's military hospitals not only left no mark on the state, but moved, taking with them their personal records and recollections. There were two notable exceptions: George Martin Kober and William Henry Corbusier. Dr. Kober kept meticulous records, then published his reminiscences.[1] Although Kober served at Fort McDermit, his most notable contributions to our history were made while he lived in the northeast corner of the Great Basin at Fort Bidwell. Dr. Corbusier, on the other hand, is indebted to his wife, Fanny Dunbar

Corbusier, for keeping a journal of her experiences
as a military surgeon's wife at Fort McDermit.[2]

19th-Century Medical Practitioners, will concen-
trate on the other intrepid practitioners who lived
in our area, and who often gave their lives to care
for their patients. Many people have given me bits
and pieces, and larger chunks of information to
identify these individuals and their contributions
to Nevada medicine.

These include first and foremost, Eileen Barker
who for many years was my co-worker at the University of Nevada School of Medicine. Eileen not
only was my research assistant, but she traveled to
remote Nevada counties to review public records.
Her thoroughness and attention to detail prevented
mistakes to which a work of this type can produce.
She also handled the correspondence, maintained
our records, organized the oral histories and mem-
oirs, and provided valuable editing.

I am also indebted to Phyllis Cudek who
researched and eloquently recorded the importance
of midwifery to early Nevada.

Edward T. Morman, Medical History Librarian at
Johns Hopkins University, was the major influence
behind the idea of this compendium. His sugges-
tion that I look at non-military medical practitioners for comparison with the Army surgeons led to
the research that began this project.[3]

Nevada State Archivist Guy Louis Rocha was invaluable with his knowledge of Nevada historiography, and he also read the manuscript and offered suggestions. Mr. Rocha, using the technology of e-mail, responded instantaneously to my inquiries regarding the history of Nevada, and he became a good friend.

A special thanks is due Sue Fawn Chung at the University of Nevada, Las Vegas who graciously read my chapter on Chinese medicine and offered criticism and information. Her knowledge of Chinese midwives at the turn of the century was particularly revealing.

Patricia A. Barry of Fort Bidwell, California, an English teacher and historian, provided me with valuable editorial comment. A stanza of one of her poems graces this work and sets the tone for the Indian medicine man.

My daughter, Kristin D. Sohn, also gave invaluable advice, and final editing was accomplished by Karen Cavallaro, Production Manager of *Greasewood Tablettes* who finished the task I started.

Most of all, this book is dedicated to those hundreds of forgotten, medical practitioners who took care of their patients when Nevada was a barren, frontier wilderness.

Anton P. Sohn
Reno, Nevada

[1] George Martin Kober, *Reminiscences of George Martin Kober, M.D., LL.D.* (Menasha, Wisc.: George Banta Pub. Co., 1930). Dr. Kober became dean of Georgetown Medical College, Washington, D.C.

[2] William T. Corbusier, *Verde to San Carlos: Recollections of a Famous Army Surgeon and His Observant Family on the Western Frontier, 1869-1886* (Tucson: Dale Stuart King, 1969) and Fanny D. Corbusier, "Recollections of Her Life in the Army," (Personal Diary).

[3] The account of the military doctors in the Great Basin is: Anton P. Sohn, *A Saw, Pocket Instruments, and Two Ounces of Whiskey: Frontier Military Medicine in the Great Basin* (Spokane, Wash.: Authur H. Clark, 1997).

CHAPTER ONE

Introduction to Nevada Medicine[1]

Until the Comstock Lode mining discovery in 1859, the territory comprising the present state of Nevada was little more than crisscrossed trails to California and Oregon. Before the Comstock strike, an estimated 7,000 Indians were the major inhabitants in the area, making the medicine man the most important—and maybe the only—medical practitioner in the area.[2] By the start of the Civil War, immigrants were beginning to settle in the territory, advancing the frontier to its remote valleys and mountains. The settlement of the West and the part of the Utah Territory which was to become the State of Nevada were protected by United States Army units. Military surgeons established Army hospitals—the first hospitals in the area—primarily to provide medical care for soldiers, but to serve all, including civilians and, in rare instances, Native Americans.[3]

Coincidental with the military presence designed to enforce peace with the Indians, mining and ranching communities were growing. Trauma in the mines and on the open range, and epidemics of smallpox, measles, scarlet fever, and infectious diarrhea necessitated increased health care for the sick and injuried. To compound the problem, the presence of miners and cowboys who lacked family support caused traditional medical care to move from the home; hospitals became a necessity.

The Civil War briefly interrupted the flood of settlers to the West, but the quest for wealth and adventure west of the Rockies could not be denied. In 1865 the war was over, and the nation again turned to its Manifest Destiny, advancing the frontier across the western deserts. More forts were established to protect travelers and homesteaders from increasingly bold Indian attacks.

In addition to settlers and miners, Chinese laborers were immigrating via coastal cities, primarily San Francisco and Seattle, to work in the mining districts and build the railroads. They brought with them traditional Chinese doctors who were well versed in the treatment of disease by use of herbal/animal concoctions proven effective by thousands of years of use. In some communities the "China Doctor" was the most important health care provider for both the Chinese and their new neighbors.

The formation of the mining districts in the West was far more than a vast unprecedented movement and settlement of the mankind. Intertwined with the Civil War it was a profound sweeping drama of unmatched magnitude. For thousands it was the adventure and opportunity of a lifetime. For many it was a tragic mistake.

Mines created conditions where penniless citizens could make a new start next to wealthy investors, downtrodden immigrants could find new homes and occupations, unschooled laborers could work next to educated physicians, and all-comers could feel welcome. Great fortunes were made and lost. The great city of San Francisco was built and the great state of Nevada was founded.

During this period when the mining districts were being formed 19th-century medicine in America was in a state of flux. Not all those who called themselves physicians were educated in the healing arts. Licensing laws were virtually non-existent and educational requirements had not yet been established to ensure that all physicians were trained. As a result, the title "doctor" included regular, irregular (homeopathic and eclectic) physicians, herbal doctors, quacks, and others. Some who had not attended any medical school simply advertised their healing skills and called themselves doctors.

During this period of turmoil in the medical profession, the cause of infectious disease, the most prevalent illness on the frontier, was elucidated— bacteria were discovered. This opened the door and allowed the search for effective cures. Before the age of bacteria, the only definitive treatment for an infectious disease was the use of quinine to treat malaria, a prevalent ailment brought to the Nevada frontier from endemic areas.

Not to be underestimated was the role of home remedies and midwives on the frontier. Many of the new citizens brought with them remedies from the old country, others borrowed from their neighbors, and still others used Native American practices. Furthermore, many of the transplanted Americans had no choice but to rely on home care on the isolated frontier where doctors were not always available. In many cases midwives provided urgently needed medical services. They not only delivered babies, they also became the community "doctor."

Therefore, in 19th-century Nevada, care for the sick and wounded was provided by five kinds of practitioners: Indian medicine men, military surgeons, Chinese doctors, assorted physicians, and midwives.

In addition to outlining the roles that various diverse culture groups contributed to wellness in their Nevada, it is the intent of this book to emphasize that these cultures had effective health systems. Too often we hear about the contributions of western medicine and do not recognize our debt to traditional healers who not only practiced mythical and empirical medicine, but used effective techniques (observation, trial, and error) and a pharmacopoeia (drugs and herbs) for thousands of years. Many of their drugs and methods were later incorporated into our therapeutic arsenal.

The China doctor and Indian medicine man were produced by long periods of rigorous training and education. They chose their profession because they demonstrated skill, interest, and the gentleness necessary to become a medical practitioner. They were dedicated to their practice even though they were often socially ostracized, and sometimes practiced their profession while threatened with death.

The China doctor and Indian medicine man also practiced holistic medicine. The philosophy of holistic medicine has recently become popular, but treatment of the whole person has always been part of the Native American culture in the Great Basin. Wellness consisted of being in harmony with one's surroundings, relatives, and friends. In Native American society, physical disease is caused by an imbalance in one's physical, psychological, or spiritual being. Healing is brought about by restoring this balance. Chanting and singing by the medicine man was one method used to help restore rhythm. In Chinese medicine, disease is also based on an imbalance in the body's systems and healing occurs with restoration of the negative *(yin)* and positive *(yang)* principles.

Here, is the story of the 19th-century medical practitioner in Nevada.

[1] Many of the stories and events in this book have been published in *Greasewood Tablettes*, the quarterly bulletin published by the History of Medicine Program at the University of Nevada School of Medicine.

[2] The earliest known non-Indian doctor to settle in the territory was Dr. T. A. Hylton at Mormon Station in 1851, but it is unknown how long he stayed or whether he practiced medicine. In 1852 Dr. Benjamin L. King located in Eagle Valley near what would become Carson City.

[3] Sohn, *A Saw, Pocket Instruments, and Two Ounces of Whiskey*.

CHAPTER TWO

Nevada's Civilian Hospitals

When the Army established a military post, the first order of business, concurrent with construction of living quarters, was the building of the hospital. When new settlers came into an area, their priorities differed from the Army's. First, the new inhabitants built homes, established businesses, and secured supplies. Unless there was an epidemic or the indigent needed care, the building of a hospital on the frontier was relegated to the bottom of a long list of necessities.

Therefore, during the frontier period, most nursing care was provided in the home by family members. Occasionally, when the need arose, local homes or buildings were turned into hospitals to care for the sick.[1] Such a situation frequently occurred when smallpox or other epidemics struck communities across Nevada.

The Beginning (Washoe and Storey County)
One of the first known hospitals in the eastern foothills of the Sierra Nevada was established in 1862 by Dr. Joseph Ellis at Steamboat Springs. It accommodated 34 patients. In contrast to an epidemic motivation, most likely this hospital was

built to take advantage of the healing properties of the springs. Unfortunately, Dr. Ellis' title to the land was disputed, and in 1867 the court awarded legal right to the property to Charles W. Cullins. Shortly thereafter, Ellis' improvements were burned to the ground, probably due to arson.[2]

In 1862 a hospital was established in the nearby Washoe Valley community of Watson's Mill; a smallpox epidemic induced the local government to levy a 20¢ tax on each $100 of property value to raise money for care of the sick.[3] Also in 1862 the Territory Legislature levied a poll tax of $4.00 per year on every man under the age of 50 to provide care for the indigent sick. The collected money was apportioned to each county so that the county commissioners could buy medical care for indigent patients. This act resulted in the establishment of indigent hospitals and "poor farms" in many counties.

The "poor farm" was adjacent to the hospital and provided work opportunity and recreation for patients who were able to work, and produce food. A similar situation existed in the 19th-century U.S. Army where the base surgeon was responsible for the hospital vegetable garden.

The epidemic in Washoe Valley continued unabated, and in 1864 the county commissioners purchased the Printing Office Building in Washoe City for $1,000 and converted it into a hospital. The county administrators awarded a contract for $2.50 a day to Dr. A. G. Weed to treat, feed, and provide medicine for the patients.[4]

Over the mountain from Washoe Valley in Storey County, site of the Comstock boom, Drs. Thomas H. Pinkerton and J. C. Tucker received a contract for $2,000 per month to provide care—food, medicine, personnel, and housing—for county patients. In 1862 the Storey County Hospital in Virginia City consisted of two buildings: one to house up to 60 male patients and a second for 14 female patients. The insane were hospitalized in the basement.[5]

Miners were also concerned about their health needs. Their principal disorders were scurvy, rheumatism, dysentery, malarial fevers (intermittent, remittent and continued), and the growing menace of trauma in mine shafts.[6] In the 1860s at least one person a week was killed, and many more were injured in the mines of the Comstock. In a 30 year period over 600 were killed in these mines.[7] Accidents from working with "rotten rock," fires resulting from explosions, and scaldings were common occurrences.[8]

On the Comstock, in the lower levels of the mine shafts, the miners encountered water temperatures of 170 degrees which caused severe burns.[9] To cope with the danger in the mines and their socio-economic situation, the miners established a Miners' League (labor organization) in 1863.[10] Beside demanding higher wages and better working conditions, their efforts were directed at providing sick, injury, and death benefits.[11] One dollar a month of each member's dues was set aside to pay for care in the existing hospitals in Virginia City.[12]

The *City Directory of 1863* lists two hospitals in Virginia City: the private hospital of Dr. William S. Minneer, located in the "Canyon," and the hospital owned by Pinkerton and Tucker. In addition, at least two other hospitals existed in Virginia City during the 1860s. Listed in the 1864-1865 business directory is La Charite Hospital staffed by the Sisters of Charity with Dr. C. B. F. Voight in charge. Later, the Sisters provided nursing care at Saint Mary Louise Hospital. The second hospital was Hospital Saint Vincent de Paul.

Journalist Alfred Doten in 1868 described surgery at Hospital Saint Vincent de Paul. Dr. Frederick Hiller, a homeopathic physician, did all of the surgery at the hospital described by Doten in his journals. Typical patients and their problems were described. For example, in April Mrs. Chubbuck came in with a thumb abscess that was "poorly treated" by another physician two months previous. Hiller took 15 minutes to amputate the arm above the elbow. One month later Mr. Peterson jammed his ankle. The pain quickly left when Dr.

Hiller produced a lance, but he nevertheless made an incision for future suppuration. Also that month, Hiller removed smashed bone from William Neely's right shoulder. This procedure took 30 minutes and Doten gave the chloroform.[13]

In the following decade (1876) Saint Mary Louise Hospital was built in Virginia City. Named for Marie Louise Bryant Mackay, the hospital was a brick, three-story structure with three wards capable of holding 50 patients. It cost $45,000 to build after the property was purchased and donated by Mrs. Mackay.[14] Her husband, John W. Mackay who had "made it big" in the mines provided substantial financial backing. The Catholic order of the Daughters of Charity from Emmitsburg, Maryland, provided the nursing care.[15]

Sister Ann Sebastian Warns and her staff of five sisters from the order worked in Saint Mary Louise Hospital, assisting Dr. John Grant, the highly qualified resident physician who had attended Albany Medical College, Jefferson Medical College and the Royal College of surgeons in London. Other physicians also practiced in the hospital.

The miners' union tax of one dollar per month also helped support Saint Mary Louise Hospital, the most modern hospital in the state and probably in the West. This union tax prevailed in many Nevada mining communities well into the 20th century and guaranteed physician and hospital care for miners.[16] Records of Saint Mary Louise Hospital show that an average of two patients a week were treated over a 20-year period, although, at times the wards were full.

Admitting diagnoses included alcoholism, trauma, fever, general debility, rheumatism and scalding from hot water in the mines. The hospital, located at 55 North R Street, had a smaller "pest" hospital for contagious diseases located behind the main structure.[17] In later years the "pest" hospital became the laundry. The hospital, at one time the pride of Virginia City, closed in 1897 when Storey County's economy declined. The building remains today, down the hill from the center of town.

Ormsby, White Pine, and Lincoln Counties

By 1874 Ormsby County, White Pine County, and Carson City had county hospitals. George H. Thoma was the White Pine County Physician.[18] Lincoln County also had a hospital constructed on the "poor farm" where a local physician received the contract to care for the indigent patients. In 1875, Simeon L. Lee, a graduate of the Physio-Medical Institute of Cincinnati, was in charge of the Lincoln County Hospital in Pioche, Nevada.[19]

Elko County

An epidemic of smallpox forced the construction of a hospital in the railroad town of Elko. In 1869 the community built a regular hospital at Third and

Railroad street and a "pest" hospital on the edge of town. Later that year, county commissioners obtained competitive bids from interested doctors— H. P. Stewart, Louis Terry, John Meigs and James F. Manley—to operate the hospital.

Meigs won the one-year contract for $150 per month and received 30¢ a day for each patient who received medication. Meigs was also the contract doctor for the United States Indian Service. A year later, Meigs again received the county hospital contract with the stipend increased to $200 per month.[20]

In 1876 Elko County closed the hospital that was described as a "wooden fire-trap," and opened a new hospital at Sixth and Court. By 1886, the county hospital occupied the recently abandoned University of Nevada building at Ninth and College.

The Elko County Hospital denied admission to the Chinese because they were not citizens. Elko, similar to most railroad and mining communities in the West, had a sizable Chinese population who were treated by trained Chinese doctors specializing in traditional Chinese medicine. Although traditional Chinese medicine was based on the use of herbs to treat illness, some seriously ill Chinese patients required surgery and/or hospitalization.

To meet the challenge, the Chinese tong in 1873 created a two-ward Chinese hospital in Elko. Dr. Ken Fung, a graduate of the School of Medicine and Surgery in Canton, was the first resident doctor, as noted in the *Elko Independent*. Fung was trained in surgery and medicine to a degree comparable to the training received by American physicians.

Nevada Hospital for Mental Disease

The physically sick and injured required hospitalization and care, but the needs of the mentally ill had to be addressed as well. Initially, the mentally deranged who exhibited bizarre behavior were jailed. In the late 1860s, more humane measures were placed into effect, and the mentally ill were admitted to local hospitals.

In 1867 the hospitals in the state could not find rooms for the growing numbers of mentally ill patients, forcing the state to contract with the California State Hospital in Stockton, California. A legislative appropriation provided $10,000 for care in Stockton for Nevada's indigent insane. Between June 1867 and December 1868 twenty patients were sent to California. During the following two years the state allotted an additional $20,000.[21]

As the cost of care escalated, the legislature appropriated $50,000 in 1871 for buying land and erecting a building in Nevada to house the indigent insane. After investigating the cost of land and construction, the state found it would not have enough money left over for patient care so the decision was made to continue sending the patients to California. Later a less expensive alternative to the California State Hospital was found; Nevada contracted with Dr. Samuel Langdon of Stockton, California, at $9 per week ($1.29 per day) per patient, but Nevadans were concerned about the adequacy of care their fellow citizens received.[22]

In order to verify adequate care for Nevada's psychiatric patients, a special commission comprised of Dr. Alson Dawson, Mr. Granville W. Huffaker and Dr. Franklin J. White was appointed by the legislature in 1875 to visit the facility in Stockton. The commission found the building was not suitable to house patients.[23] During a five year period, medical care in California for the 150 Nevada patients had cost the state of Nevada up to $5,000 a month ($1.11 per day). However, a solution was at hand.[24]

Prior to 1879, the federal government had given land to the state, just east of Reno, to be used as a prison site. Construction of the prison was begun, but work was never completed, and the land became available for a mental hospital. The state legislature appropriated $5,000 to investigate the project. Dr. Alson Dawson presented a plan whereby two or three patients could live in small units on the state hospital grounds and receive medical care from a resident physician.

In 1881 Dr. Dawson's plan was approved, and an act provided $80,000 for the construction of several two-story buildings with enough capacity to house 200 patients. For $2,400 a year, the state hired Dr.

Dawson, the first superintendent and the resident physician.[25] On July 1, 1882, 138 patients were received by train from California and admitted to the Nevada Hospital for the Indigent Insane.

In 1883 when Dr. Simeon Bishop was the superintendent, the hospital had 140 patients, 110 of whom were men. Dr. Bishop's biennial report to the legislature listed a cost to the state of 79¢ a day per patient.[26] Most of this amount covered housing and food, and very little went to psychiatric care. In fact, many patients entered the hospital because they had no means of support.

Biennial reports to the legislature gave patient names, diagnoses, ages, and nationalities. Patient confidentiality was not deemed necessary in 19th-century Nevada. The causes of insanity of the patients were listed as: masturbation (20 percent of the men), onanism, heredity, typhoid, religion, scarlet fever, epilepsy, syphilis, fright, intemperance, jealousy, alcoholism, ardent spirits, weak mind, disappointment, loss of money, and solitary life.[27] Two thirds of the patients in 1891 were from Europe, reflecting the massive immigration and westward movement.

The humane treatment of mentally ill patients occurred at about the same time that the medical profession began to understand the etiology of disease and the bacterial cause of infections. Coincidentally, changes in medical education were occurring to ensure better trained doctors. These changes, such as graded courses and educational entrance requirements, were occurring in medical education at the turn of the century, but it would be several years before research, laboratory studies, and university affiliation would benefit psychiatric patients.

In 1895 the superintendent at the State Hospital, Dr. Henry Bergstein, advanced humane care and stopped "the custom of placing the inmates on exhibition for the amusement of and to gratify the morbid curiosity of visitors." He also changed the facility's name of "The Hospital for the Indigent Insane" to "Nevada Hospital for Mental Diseases."[28]

Nevada's hospitals moved into the 20th century with dignity.

[1] This is related by George D. Lyman to have occurred in the early 1860s in Virginia City when hundreds became sick and many died from drinking water contaminated with "arsenic, plumbago, and copperas." Subsequent research has made this an unlikely event and the story apparently was an attempt by Lyman to glamorize the memory of Julia Bulette, a well-known Virginia City prostitute who was murdered. Lyman wrote that she turned her house into a hospital where she, Father Patrick Manogue, Reverend Franklin Rising, Dr. Edmund G. Bryant, and Dr. Sheldon McMeans administered care to those poisoned. See George D. Lyman, *The Saga of the Comstock Lode: Boom Days in Virginia City* (New York: Charles Scribner's Sons, 1934) p. 90. Also read Douglas McDonald, Stanley W. Paher, ed., *The Legend of Julia Bulette and the Red light Ladies of Nevada* (Las Vegas: Nev. Pub., 1980) and Susan James, "Queen of Tarts," *Nevada* 44, no. 5 (1984) pp. 51-53.

[2] Angel, Myron, ed., with introduction by David F. Myrick, *History of Nevada with Illustrations and Biographical Sketches of its Prominent Men and Pioneers (Oakland, Calif.: Thompson & West, 1881) reissued by (Berkeley:* Howell-North, 1958) Helen J., Poulson, *Index to Thompson and West's History of Nevada,* Bibliographical Series, no. 6 (Carson City, Nev.: Univ. Nev. Press, 1966) p. 645.

[3] Carroll Ogren, "History of Washoe Medical Center," Reno, Washoe Med. Ctr.

[4] Leona M. Cox, "The Care Given to the Mentally Ill Prior to the Establishment of the Nevada State Hospital," Nursing

Seminar August 31, 1960, Reno, Univ. Nev., Special Collections, p. 7.

[5] *Ibid.*, pp. 5-6.

[6] James L. Tyson, *Diary of a Physician in California* (Oakland, Calif.: Bilbooks, 1955) p 79.

[7] Miriam Michelson, *The Wonderlode of Silver and Gold* (Boston: Stratford Co., 1934), p 167.

[8] The worse mine disaster in the West was a fire in the Yellow Jacket at Gold Hill on April 7, 1869, where 45 were killed. Richard E. Lingenfelter, *The Hardrock Miners* (Berkeley, Calif.: Univ. Calif. Press, 1974) p. 26.

[9] It has been shown that water with a temperature as low as 112° Fahrenheit can burn the skin.

[10] Michelson, *The Wonderlode of Silver and Gold*, p. 170. This attempt at forming a union failed and on December 8, 1866, the model union was formed in the town of Gold Hill. (Lingenfelter, *The Hardrock Miners*, p. 43).

[11] Lingenfelter, *The Hardrock Miners*, pp. 27, 51, and 52.

[12] *Ibid.*, p. 52.

[13] Alfred Doten, *The Journals of Alfred Doten: 1849-1903*, vols. I-III Walter Van Tilburg Clark, ed. (Reno: Univ. Nev. Press, 1973) pp. 986-1008 passim.

[14] See Appendix I, Edmund G. Bryant.

[15] Mrs. Mackey's first husband, Dr. Edmund G. Bryant, died earlier in La Porte, California, from alcoholism.

[16] Anton P. Sohn, "Dr. Gerald J. Sylvain Oral History," Reno, Nev., Path. Depart., Univ. Nev. School Med., 1991. The custom was still observed in 1934 when Dr. Sylvain practiced in Goldfield, Nev.

[17] "Pest" is derived from pestilence.

[18] John F. Uhlhorn, *Virginia and Truckee Railroad Directory 1873-74* (Sacramento: 1873) and Samuel W. Butler, *The Medical Register and Directory of the United States* (Philadelphia: Office Med. Surg. Reporter, 1877).

[19] Simeon L. Lee, Nat. Lib. Med., Box 3, MS C 142. See Lee letter applying for the position of Military Surgeon in the Nevada National Guard, Appendix V.

[20] Edna B. Patterson, *Sagebrush Doctors and Health Conditions of Northeast Nevada from Aboriginal Times to 1972* (Springville, Utah: Utah Art City Pub. Co., 1972) pp. 61-68. Army doctors during this period made $120 a month plus room and board.

[21] Cox, *The Care Given to the Mentally Ill*, pp. 16-23.

[22] *Ibid.*, p.25.

[23] Alson W. and Lillian Dawson, *Greener Grass* (Boise: Dawson House, 1984) p. 36.

[24] Cox, *The Care Given to the Mentally Ill*, pp. 25-33.

[25] *Ibid.*, pp. 33-35.

[26] Biennial Report of the Commissioners and Superintendent, *Indigent Insane of Nevada* (Carson City, Nev.: 1883-1884).

[27] *Ibid.*, (1889-1890).

[28] *Ibid.*, (1895-1896). The custom of allowing casual visitors to go to the mental hospital for entertainment dates to 1770 in London. The practice probably began at Bethlem Hospital, commonly known as Bedlam, where a fee was charged for the curious to "laugh at the lunatics." Kathleen Jones, *Asylums and After* (London: Athlone Press, 1993) p. 9.

CHAPTER THREE

Native American Doctors

Introduction

If one only considers those diseases or "whiteman illnesses"—measles, malaria, tuberculosis, gonorrhea, smallpox, alcoholism, and the list goes on— that non-native inhabitants brought to the Native Americans in the West, the natives were immensely better off before their country was invaded. Life was harsh on the Great Basin, and starvation was a threat, but the inhabitants were free of alcoholism and these infectious diseases.[1]

In this chapter the medical practices of the native inhabitants and how they dealt with both their diseases and disease brought by the newcomers will be discussed. Although their health system is unique, it shared practices with other cultures. Native American medical practices will be compared to 19th-century medicine—military, civilian, Chinese and folk practices.

In order to understand Native American medical practices in the Great Basin, a definition of this area according to the Native American groups who lived in it is needed. Anthropologists divide the 19th-century Great Basin into nine tribal-territorial groups. Obviously, the Native American tribes were not aware of these boundaries and there was considerable overlap, not only in territory, but also in culture. Furthermore, many of the tribes were nomadic and roamed the Great Basin, and others spent considerable time outside of its mountainous boundary. Even though the territories were fluid and the groups intermarried, each retained its separate culture.

The nine tribal groups of the Intermountain West were Western Shoshone, Northern Shoshone/Bannock, Eastern Shoshone, Ute, Southern Paiute, Kawaiisu, Owens Valley Paiute, Northern Paiute, and Washoe.[2] However, virtually all of the Northern Shoshone/Bannock, Eastern Shoshone, Ute, and Southern Paiute actually lived outside of the area topographically defined as the Great Basin.[3] Furthermore, only four tribes—Washoe, Northern Paiute, Southern Paiute, and Washoe—inhabited Nevada. Two—the Owens Valley Paiute and the Kawaiisu—lived on the southern border with California, but they interacted with the Nevada tribes. All of these groups had distinct and separate practices, but they dealt with disease and doctors in a similar fashion. It is important to keep in mind that they not only respected each other's practices, but they borrowed from each other as well.

Western Shoshone

The Western Shoshone occupied the largest Nevada territory which extended from the depths of arid Death Valley and adjacent Panamint Mountains, north to the Idaho border, and east to include the Great Salt Lake. Most of this area was sparsely inhabited and, in fact, was the last area in the United States where settlers displaced the resident Native Americans. The Army moved them to reservations and established Forts Halleck and Ruby to keep the peace in the western half of Western Shoshone territory.

Washoe

The Washoe occupied the lake area of the Sierra Nevada to the north and south of Lake Tahoe and the neighboring valleys on the western slope of the Great Basin. Although the Washoe predated the other tribes in the region and belonged to a different language group, they shared many beliefs with their neighbors.

Kawaiisu

The Kawaiisu were located in California, in a small area on the southern border of Nevada. They were more closely associated with their California neighbors than with other Great Basin Native Americans.

Owens Valley Paiute

Similar to the Kawaiisu, the Owens Valley Paiute lived on the southwestern rim of the Great Basin in a small, stable, non-nomadic community that bordered on Nevada.

Southern Paiute

Southern Paiute territory extended from a corner of California across both Southern Nevada and Southern Utah into Northern Arizona. There were few immigrant settlements and no permanent military bases in the Nevada part of the Southern Paiute territory.

Northern Paiute

In contrast to the stability of the Owens Valley Paiute, Washoe, and Kawaiisu, the Northern Paiute people consisted of seminomadic groups that seasonally occupied parts of the Western Great Basin, extending from the Owens Valley in the south, across Nevada to Oregon on the north, and west to the Humboldt River. Their territory consisted of the western half of Nevada. In this area the Army established most of its larger military installations: Forts Churchill, Scott, McDermit, McGarry, Bidwell, Warner, Harney, and several dozen smaller temporary encampments.

Ute

The Great Basin territory of the Ute comprised a small part of the middle of Utah, extending south of the Great Salt Lake. Most of the Ute territory was outside the Great Basin and extended further east into Colorado. Only rarely did they venture into Nevada.

Health System

Native American's health system dealt with health, rites of passage—birth, naming, puberty, disease, and death—old age, and mental illness. Many individuals in the various tribes were part of this coordinated and coherent system which had a rich and strongly conservative tradition that was developed over a 10,000 year tradition.

The women of the tribe oversaw the birth process and menstrual rites, although on occasion a shaman might be called during a difficult birth.

The cause and treatment of diseases experienced by Great Basin Native Americans, which is the topic of this chapter, was a complex issue mainly as a result of the close link between medicine and religion. A healthy individual had a harmonious relationship with the supernatural, while disease was result of a disturbance in this balance. Healing, brought about in one of several manners, re-established the balance, and the medicine man was instrumental in the process.

Health Providers

Generally, there were two classes of health providers—the herbalist and the medicine man/

shaman. The herbalist treated minor ailments, such as broken bones, minor trauma, indigestion, etc. He or she mixed concoctions and had knowledge of plants and herbs. In some tribes they practiced bloodletting. On another level, the medicine man or shaman had varying degrees of power. The medicine man had considerably less power than the shaman, who healed while in a deep trance. In this mode the shaman went on soul journeys and rescued the soul of his patient.

Herbalist

Most injury and common minor illness were not considered to be caused by a supernatural phenomenon and were treated with herbs and home remedies similar to folk medicine as practiced by the non-native American citizens. To accomplish this task, various members of the tribe, usually women, gathered the plants during the appropriate seasons, dried them, and pulverized them for later use. Of note, and as pointed out later, is the fact that several of the plants used in modern pharmacology were used by Native North Americans.

Of all the Native American groups in the Great Basin, the Western Shoshone had the greatest knowledge of plants and their medicinal uses, and they carefully guarded this information. In contrast, the Washoe Indians had little knowledge and bought their herbs from neighboring California tribes.[4] Fifty-two plants were used by the Western

Shoshone for upper respiratory disease, 57 for venereal disease, 44 for swelling, 34 for diarrhea, 37 for rheumatism, and 48 for stomach disorders.[5] The large number of herbs used for these various conditions is a manifestation of the empirical philosophy of their health system. The Chinese had similar practices, but in addition they used animal parts in their concoctions.

Shamanism

More serious illnesses required treatment by a medicine man/shaman. Some healed while in a light trance; others experienced a deeper spell. Only in a deep trance could a shaman leave his body, become ecstatic, and rescue the soul of the sick person, who was usually suffering from a disease with altered consciousness such as coma or delirium. Furthermore, a shaman was either a generalist with general curing ability or a specialist with ability to cure a specific disease such as a rattlesnake bite.

Laying-on of hands was also an important part of the shaman's ritual. This practice is similar to the Christian practice of healing by laying-on of hands, an important psychological factor in healing. Modern medicine would recognize the shaman as a psychotherapist.

Central to the shaman's medical practice was the concept that disease was caused by the intrusion of an object within the body. The Western Shoshone believed that an arrow-shooting dwarf caused disease.[6] During the healing ritual the shaman sucked out the foreign object, which may have been a stick or blood, and displayed it for all to see. On the other hand, disease was sometimes blamed on a transgression or the soul leaving the body.

At the conclusion of this healing ceremony, the members of the tribe required positive results—improvement in the condition of the patient. Furthermore, they believed that evil medicine doctors or sorcerers practiced witchcraft and caused disease. These were identified as shamans who too often failed to invoke a cure or refused to treat a patient.

This was a serious charge, and there was an unwritten law that if a shaman had three patients die, the shaman would be put to death—malpractice punishment at its extreme. At Fort Ruby, a shaman lost his third patient and members of the Shoshone tribe decided to kill him. Mr. Wines, a local rancher who was trusted, called the tribe members together and informed them that he would send for the soldiers if they murdered the shaman. A compromise was reached and the Shoshones returned to their wikiups with a guarantee from the shaman that he would give up the practice of medicine.[7]

The *Inyo Independence* poignantly emphasized the shamans' accountability in 1876 when measles killed many in the Owens Valley Paiute community. The tribe, in turn, killed more than 80 of its medicine men and their sons for practicing witch-craft.[8] Thus, many of their traditions died, and little is known of their medical practices.

During the epidemic Dr. Washington Matthews from nearby Fort Independence offered help, but the Owens Valley Paiute were suspicious of non-native medicine. The following year a smallpox epidemic hit the Owens Valley. By then, they would accept help, and Dr. Matthews provided vac-cination. Ten years later in 1887, there were 776 Native Americans in the valley, reduced by disease to a third of its size before the military occupation.[9]

The Northern Paiute also dealt with repeated unsatisfactory results by killing the medicine man.[10] Patricia Barry's family has lived for over a hundred years in northern Modoc County in the village of Fort Bidwell. She recalls such an episode.

Sometime in the late 1800s or early 1900s, the Warner Valley-Surprise Valley Paiutes' Sing Doctor Noah or Doc Noey, failed in a cure and lost his patient. This apparently was at or near Fort Bidwell. Noah fled in fear for his life, but the patient's relatives pursued him into Warner Valley and attacked him with knives. According to oral tradition among both Indians and whites, Noah was knifed, resulting in a cut across his abdomen from hipbone to hipbone.

Some whites found Noah lying alongside the road and took him to the Adel Store. He was placed upon the store counter and sympathetic men cleansed the wound, then proceeded to sew up the damage with sack twine and a needle. It was not said whether the wound was bound, but Noah is supposed to have been dressed in clean clothes.

He recovered and lived to be a revered old man. In the end, his losing the patient only added to his charisma because it was felt by the local Indians that no one could survive an abdominal knife wound.[11]

Furthermore, contrary to what many local people still say shamanism was alive and well among the Fort Bidwell Paiutes into the late 1940's. The drumming-singing rituals were clearly audible by the white community.[12] The Kawaiisu name for the curing shaman was *huviyagadi* (one who has a song). Similar to other tribes of the Great Basin, laying-on of hands, blowing smoke and removing a foreign object were important.[13]

In the Owens Valley Paiute culture, the shaman had another role in addition to healing. He figured prominently in the social context of the community, and was called on to give advice and arbitrate disputes.[14]

Medical Education

There were several ways an individual could become a shaman—heredity, through a dream, and by visiting sacred sites. An individual could become a shaman in the Northern Paiute culture by any of these three methods. Power *(puha)* to heal could be inherited from a parent (either sex and usually deceased), acquired in a dream, or deliberately sought by visiting designated caves considered to hold *puha*. After spending a night in such a cave, the neophyte shaman would spend two or three years in preparation, and would usually be apprenticed to a practicing shaman, to learn the secrets and methods of curing.[15] An American citizen could also become a doctor by serving an apprenticeship without formal education.

A shaman's specific power also could be acquired through a dream in which he saw himself curing a patient who had the same problem in which he would later specialize.[16] By all of these described methods the shaman created a relationship with the spirit world. The Washoe shaman's relationship with the spirit power was known as *(wegeléyu)*. After this power manifested itself to an individual, it took three to five years under a senior shaman to become a shaman.

The Healing Ritual

Each shaman practiced the healing ritual in his distinct and unique manner, but sagebrush was usually a common denominator in the process. In a Western Shoshone healing ritual the shaman piled sagebrush around a fire pit and placed the sick person on the pile of sage. The shaman sang and meditated, and then placed his mouth on the area and sucked out the pain. If the illness was more serious, the shaman gave a longer treatment with chanting and singing, fasting, making sacrifices, and more importantly, using sacred eagle feathers.

In another healing ceremony, the shaman drew lines with a sacred diatomaceous rock (*abve*) on his patient and instructed the patient to go to the river early the next day to sprinkle water, pray and make a sacrifice.[17]

In a Southern Shoshone ritual, the shaman lay beneath the patient and removed the disease- producing object by sucking.[18] Both the Southern Paiute and Northern Shoshone used chanting/singing and drumming/dancing in their ceremony.

In a Washoe ritual the healing ceremony took place over four nights and was open to the public. With the patient's head to the west, the shaman blew smoke over the body. He then danced and sucked out an "object" or blew a whistle to invoke the cure. Sometimes the shaman passed out and then coughed up the object, holding it out for all to see. The patient was washed and rubbed with sage.

Military surgeon George Martin Kober described some of the Northern Paiute practices at Fort Bidwell. He wrote that they used internal and external herbs, dry cupping, and scarification for some inflammatory conditions. He witnessed the application of hot, dry stones on the umbilicus to treat hysteria. The Indians treated rattlesnake bite with sucking, ligature, and a poultice of chopped lupine.[19] These treatments were used by the ordinary Indian doctor, but the shaman practiced on a higher plane by rescuing the soul.

In the Northern Paiute culture the process of curing took two days and began when relatives of the sick person visited the shaman. The shaman smoked and meditated, then he or an assistant placed an eagle feather on a willow shaft outside the dwelling of the sick person to inhibit evil influence. That evening, the shaman placed the head of the patient and the eagle feather to the south. At dusk, he sang to acquire *puha* and sometimes he chose a person to dance through the night.

If the cure didn't work the shaman prescribed a second night of treatment or called another shaman. The ceremony often involved sucking the affected part and disposing of the disease-producing object. To finish the healing process he might prescribe food or herbs.

Healing Objects Used by the Shaman

Various paraphernalia used by the medicine doctor had religious and healing power. Although most were crude or simple items—a cane, body paint, eagle claw, deer dewclaw, pipe, rattle, or even a stone—they gave great, supernatural power to the healer. Many Great Basin tribes used a medicine pouch containing similar items.

Healing objects of the Southern Paiute medical profession were cocoon rattles made under the guidance of a dream, eagle feathers bound with

buckskin, and other various items, such as minia-
ture baskets, stone mortars, bird-bone whistles,
tobacco pouches, and stone pipes. Also, elaborate
costumes with red and white body paint, decorative
headdresses, and personal ornaments were worn by
the shaman.

Hydrotherapy

In addition to shamanism and herbs, the Nevada
Indian believed in hydrotherapy. Since ancient
times, the Western Shoshone used water from
Medicine Springs in eastern Ruby Valley to cure
various ailments. On occasion, family groups
camped near the springs to use its curative water.
When necessary, they carried the spring water to
distant camps for use by the afflicted.[20]

The Northern Paiute also practiced hydrotherapy. Near Fort Harney in Beulah Valley were several hot springs that were used by the Native
Americans. The ranchers in the area believed the
high incidence of pneumonia and pulmonary disease among the Native Americans was due to their
bathing in the springs during cold weather.[21]

Hydrotherapy also had advocates among 19th-
century Euro-Americans. Genoa, the earliest settlement in the territory that became Nevada, had
Genoa Hot Springs whose waters cured "rheumatic,
cutaneous and scrofulous affections." The spring, a
short distance south of Carson City, offered hot and
cold water, mud, and vapor baths. The healing

process was supervised by a physician who helped with proper drugs and concoctions.[22]

Another form of hydrotherapy used by the American Indian involved the use of the sweat house by the shaman. A small brush hut was made air-tight with mud, and he placed the patient inside. Water thrown on hot rocks produced steam while a shaman and an assistant sang and smoked a pipe. Sometimes the shaman buried the disease beneath hot rocks, while at other times he buried it in ashes under a fire by thrusting his bare hands through the hot ashes, thereby producing a cure.[23] Again, there were similarities in Western culture. North European cultures used the Finnish sauna or steam room for healing or cleansing the body. The significant difference between Native American sweat houses and the Old World sauna is that the former stressed cleansing of the soul or spirit.

Tobacco

Various kinds of "tobacco" were used by the Great Basin Indian. The Kawaiisu used a relative of the eastern tobacco plant while many Paiute smoked leaves from "Indian tobacco" which is more commonly called curly dock (*Rumex crispus*) or sour dock. The leaves and seeds of this plant, which are rich in vitamin C were also eaten.

Tobacco was smoked by western Native Americans for ritualistic, medicinal, and religious purposes. Limited to small amounts on infrequent occasions, it is doubtful that there were any harmful effects to the natives who inhaled the smoke through the nose. It remained for the new immigrants to abuse and spread the habit throughout the world.

Today, the World Health Organization estimates that approximately 750 million individuals will have significant health problems from the use of cigarettes.[24] This could be considered the Indians' revenge for the introduction of the many infectious diseases by the new inhabitants to the Native Americans.

Members of the Kawaiisu tribe placed particular magic and curative powers in the use of tobacco. Two species of tobacco grew in their area: *Nicotiana attenuata*, a native of the Great Basin, and *N. bigelovii*, a native of California.[25]

Mixtures of these tobaccos and herbs were believed to have magical and medicinal powers. They were used internally as an emetic and soporific. Externally, they relieved pain, cured skin conditions, and stopped bleeding.

In addition to tobacco, the Kawaiisu believed in three other primary medicines: jimsonweed, nettle, and red ants. A ball of live red ants mixed with eagle down was swallowed to cure gastrointestinal, kidney, and blood disorders. To cure other diseases the Kawaiisu utilized counter-irritation, a principle of treatment also used in Western and Oriental cultures.[26]

Fees of the Medicine Doctor

The usual fee for a curing ceremony consisted of animal hides or beads which were a token to establish a relationship. If the healing ceremony did not produce a cure, the fee would sometimes be returned.

In the Washoe culture the family usually paid the fee—buckskin, ornaments, or baskets—in advance. (The Washoe were the expert basket makers of the Great Basin.) Then, at the end of the cure, a feast was held. If the patient was not cured or died, the pay was returned. Then, the family hired another shaman to neutralize the sorcery of the first shaman. They also had the right to kill the unsuccessful shaman.[27]

Summary

This description of the medical practices of the various Great Basin tribes demonstrates similar practices used by widely separated family groups. Their white neighbors also borrowed some of their practices. Several Indian herbs—valerian, ephedra, and ergot—were adopted into our pharmacopoeia. Chemical analysis has found pharmacologically active ingredients and led to isolation and synthesis of related compounds. In a new industry called "chemical prospecting," current researchers are studying the plants growing and used in the Great Basin by native inhabitants. Dr. Ronald Pardini at the University of Nevada School of Medicine investigated the antineoplastic properties of the greasewood or creosote bush *(genus Larrea).*[28] This plant is the oldest known bush in the Great Basin.

Many of the herbal methods used by these Native American doctors were effective. However, many cures sold to the American public by other "doctors" or purveyors of patent medicine had no efficacy. Also, Native American medicine placed a strong emphasis on the psychology of healing, a potent ingredient in the healing process.

The Native American doctor provided a service to his patient that compared favorably to medical care delivered to the average American during the period of frontier medicine in the West.

---

[1] Pneumonia, starvation, and exposure were the most common threats to the Native American's existence.

[2] Warren L., *Great Basin, Handbook of North American Indians*, vol. 11 (Wash., D.C.: Smithsonian Inst., 1986) p. ix.

[3] Bill Fiero, *Geology of the Great Basin* (Reno: Univ. Nev. Press, 1986) pp. 6-7.

[4] Percy Train, James R. Henrichs and W. Andrew Archer, *Medicinal Uses of Plants by Indian Tribes of Nevada* (Lawrence, Mass.: Quarterman Pub., Rev. 1957) pp. 3-7.

[5] D'Azevedo, *Great Basin, Handbook of North American Indians*, p. 272.

[6] Hultkrantz, *The Religions of the American Indians*, p. 64.

[7] Edna B. Patterson, "Florence Wines Sharp Oral History, Elko, Nev., 1958.

[8] Dorothy Clora Cragen, *The Boys in the Sky-Blue Pants: The Men and Events at Camp Independence and Forts of Eastern California, Nevada and Utah, 1862-1877* (Fresno, Calif.: Pioneer Pub Co., 1975) p. 184.

[9] *Ibid.*, pp. 186-187.

[10] D'Azevedo, *Great Basin, Handbook of North American Indians*, pp. 451-452.

[11] Patricia Barry, Interview by the author, May 15, 1994.

[12] *Ibid.*

[13] D'Azevedo, *Great Basin, Handbook of North American Indians*, p. 406.

[14] *Ibid.*, p. 428.

[15] *Ibid.*, pp. 451-452.

[16] The spontaneous dream or vision resulting in an individual being called to practice medicine is unique to the tribes in the Western States. Åke Hultkrantz, *The Religions of the American Indians* (Berkeley, Calif.: Univ. Calif. Press, 1967) p. 75.

[17] Helen M. Blue, "An Oral History on Albina Redner: A Shoshone Life," Reno, Univ. Nev., 1990.

[18] D'Azevedo, *Great Basin, Handbook of North American Indians*, p. 383.

[19] George Martin Kober Manuscript, MS 315, Hist. Med. Div., Nat. Lib. Med., Bethesda, Md., p. 213.

[20] Patterson, *Sagebrush Doctors*, pp. 22-23.

[21] Eugene Luckey, Interview by the author, May 17, 1994.

[22] Duane A. Smith, "Comstock Miseries: Medicine and Mining in the 1860s," *Nev. Hist. Soc. Quart.*, 36, no. 1 (Sept. 1993) p. 10.

[23] Patterson, *Sagebrush Doctors*, pp. 6-7.

[24] Carlos A. Camargo, "1492—The Medical Consequences," *West. J. Med.*, 160, no. 6 (June 1994) p. 552.

[25] The principle tobacco plant used in cigarettes is *Nicotiana tabacum*, a relative of the Great Basin tobacco plants.

[26] D'Azevedo, *Great Basin, Handbook of North American Indians*, p. 403.

[27] *Ibid.*, pp. 489-490.

[28] Ronald S. Pardini et all, "Inhibition of Mitochondrial Electron Transport by Nor-Dihydroguaiaretic Acid (NDGSA)," *Biochem. Pharm.* 19 (1970) pp. 2695-2699; Carin Thomas et all, "Photoactivation of Hypericin Generates Singlet Oxygen in Mitochondria and Inhibits Succinoxidase," *Photochem. and*

Photobio. 55, no. 1 (1992) pp. 47-53; and Carin Thomas and Ronald S. Pardini, "Oxygen Dependence of Hypericin-Induced Phototoxicity to EMT6 Mouse Mammary Carcinoma Cells," *Photochem. and Photobio.* 55, no. 6 (1992) pp. 831-837.

CHAPTER FOUR

Chinese Doctors[1]

Chinese merchants and laborers came to the Great Basin through the port of San Francisco in the mid-19th century. By 1860 there were only 23 Chinese in Nevada, compared to 7,000-8,500 Native American Indians and 6,857 white immigrants. Twenty years later there were 5,416 Chinese, mostly males, in the state, accounting for 8.7 percent of the population.[2] These new immigrants worked in the mines, on the railroads and construction projects, and built the Union Pacific Railroad through the mountains and across the desert. Afterwards, national and local movements of opposition forced a marked reduction in numbers of Chinese. Even though they supplied needed services necessary for western expansion, the Chinese suffered from discrimination and had no choice but to provide their own medical and hospital care.

Fortunately, traditional herbal doctors—China Doctors or Chinese physicians—also came to America and brought a well-organized body of medical knowledge based on thousands of years of clinical trials, experiments, and careful observations.[3] Unlike American folk herbalists, they were well-

schooled in their craft and had an organized pharmacopoeia. The professional Chinese physician was
a mid-level practitioner and the backbone of medical practice in the traditional social triangle. At the
top was the scholar-physician who was usually a
member of the royal court, while at the lower end
was the "folk practitioner."

In addition to herbal medicine, Chinese medicine has a long tradition of surgery. A famous surgeon, Hua T'o, lived in the 2nd-century A.D. and
performed amputations. Today, the best known
Chinese practice is acupuncture, a practice that was
reserved for the royal court in the 19th century.

In the New World, Chinese physicians became
prominent and influential in both the Chinese and
American communities. There were several reasons for their prominence. In many mining districts there was a shortage of medical practitioners
and the Chinese physician fulfilled a need. In addition, for many illnesses Chinese medicine was
superior to Western. For example, it was more
effective in dealing with female complaints, sexual
disorders, and psychological symptoms. Furthermore, the Chinese doctor was usually highly liter-
ate and well-educated.

Dating from the 1st-century B.C., the earliest
pharmacopoeia of the professional physician, Pen-ts
áo ching, attributed to Shen-nung, contained 265
drugs classified either non-toxic and "superior" or

"inferior" and toxic which were reserved for serious illness.[4] Of the 265 drugs, 240 were vegetable substances. By the 16th century 8,160 prescriptions, made from 1,892 ingredients, were listed, and by the 20th century there were approximately 2,000 described ingredients.[5] On the American frontier, probably no more than 600 of these ingredients were available. "Doc Ing Hay" had a little over 500 herbs and animal parts in the Kam Wah Chung Pharmacy in John Day, Oregon, a gold-mining town 70 miles north of the Great Basin.[6]

Although herbs, minerals, and animal parts were important to traditional Chinese medicine, pulse diagnosis based on careful observation, was the basis of diagnosis and treatment for 19th-century patients. Using this method, the diagnosis is made by taking the pulse at three sites on each radial artery. Each site corresponds to a body organ and is further divided into a deep and superficial pulse. Thus, there is a superficial and light pulse, known as *Fu*, and a deep and bounding pulse, *Ch'en*. The third and fourth principal pulses are *Ch'ih*, a slow pulse at the rate of three beats per respiration, and *Shu*, a fast beat at six per respiration. It was said that by the use of pulsology a Chinese practitioner could describe the symptoms and past history of a patient without even seeing the patient.[7]

The number of Chinese practitioners in the Great Basin or in Nevada is difficult to count.[8]

Some advertised and had their names printed in business directories. Many registered their diploma with the county recorder as required by the law, but many did not. Furthermore, when the long arm of the law tried to prosecute them for failure to register, the jury was reluctant to convict the offender. In one instance a jury refused to convict a Chinese Doctor who did not register his diploma. It was obvious that Chinese doctors provided a service that was appreciated by the white settlers. In a community in Southern Idaho most of the white women went to Chinese doctors with whom they had better rapport than with white doctors.[9]

Not all of the practices brought by the Chinese to the Great Basin were good. They brought opium smoking and opium dens to the fast-living mining and railroad communities. In fact, in John Day, Oregon, an opium den was located in Dr. Ing Hay's home and office. Opium provided escape from a hopeless situation by dreaming about happier times in the old country, but it was not cheap.

A Chinese labor made $1 a day and spent 50¢ on opium. It has been calculated that 15-30 percent of the Chinese laborers in Nevada were addicted. Initially the habit spread to gamblers and prostitutes, but it eventually gained acceptance in the general population. To cope with the growing problem, Virginia City in 1876 passed a law against opium smoking.[10] Unfortunately, this was not enough to curtail its use in a community where any law was difficult to enforce.

Opium and related compounds were available from many sources and its use spread throughout the mining camps of Nevada during the 1870s. Opiates were even an ingredient in over-the-counter patent medicines, and the Chinese used opium to commit suicide.[11]

An overdose of opium by use of the "Black Pill," was used by Chinese workers to commit suicide. A severely injured laborer, without support of any family in this country, saw himself as a liability to his friends. Invalids were unable to return home because of the expense, and the non-Chinese offered no sympathy or support. Consequently, if the invalid Chinese could not work or perform useful services, suicide was the only way out, and it was often assisted by friends.[12]

Although the extent of this practice is unknown, opium use may be considered the dark side of the Chinese legacy in the new world. On a more positive side, many Chinese prescriptions and practices were just as effective, and in some cases had more efficacy than some of the 19th-century drugs used by American physicians on the western frontier.

It is clear that western medicine could profit from closer scrutiny of the ancient healing practices of the Chinese.

---

[1] This chapter is an over simplification of Chinese medicine, and I am not trying to convey a complete understanding of their health system.

[2] Statistics are from the Nevada State Museum in Carson City. After 1880 the total number and percentage of Chinese in Nevada steadily declined. At the turn of the century there were 1,352 Chinese, accounting for 3.2 percent of the population.

[3] The Chinese physicians brought to the U.S. by the tongs/ associations could demand passage for their wives. This is reflected in the census where their wives are listed. Also, in keeping with their training in China, physicians did research and experimentation in America, publishing their findings in San Francisco.

[4] In addition to the properties of a plant, the Chinese attached significance to the shape and color of a plant. For example, they believed yellow flowers cured jaundice, and a kidney-shaped bean was effective in renal disease.

[5] Jeffrey Barlow and Christine Richardson, *China Doctor of John Day* (Portland, Oregon: Binford & Mort, 1979) pp. 57-58.

[6] *Ibid.*, p. 98.

[7] *Ibid.*, pp. 114-58 passim.

[8] I was able to discover records dating from 1860 to 1900 of 63 Chinese doctors compared to 641 civilian doctors of European background. Using this data, Chinese doctors were 9.8 per cent of the total doctors. On the other hand, Chinese comprised approximately 6.4 per cent of the total population in Nevada. Although these statistics are rough estimates, they suggest

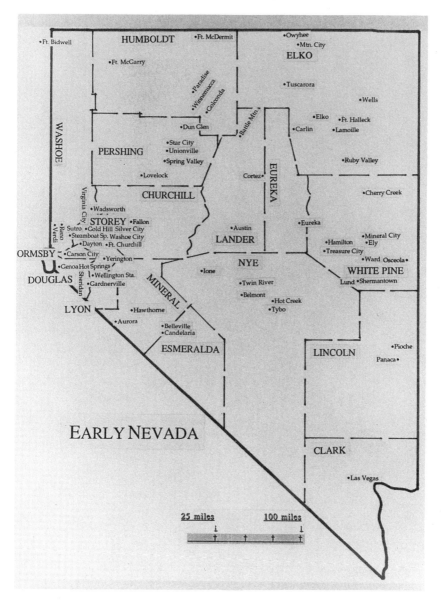

19th Century Nevada Map (Great Basin History of Medicine)

Kam Wah Chung Pharmacy, John Day, Oregon (Great Basin History of Medicine)

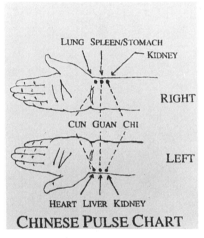

Chinese Pulse Positions (after Wallnoser and von Rottauscher)

Chinese Doctor Wai Tong (Nevada State Museum)

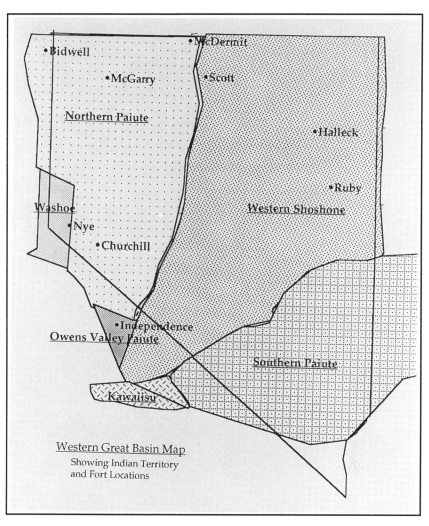

Ethnographic map of Nevada (Great Basin History of Medicine)

INDIAN TOBACCO (grows wild)
(Nicotiana attenuata)
(S) Poo-ee-pa   (P) Poo-ee-bah-mah

Though usually smoked, the dried leaves were also used in a number of external applications. They were used to treat toothaches, also eczema, cuts, hives and even snakebites.
A tea made of the leaves was also used to expel worms.

Tobacco plant (Univ. Nevada School Med. Collection)

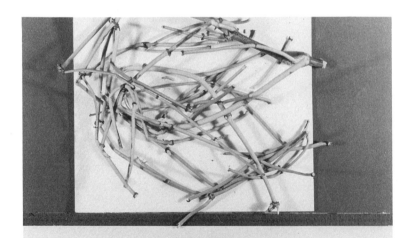

INDIAN TEA OR MORMON TEA
(Ephedra Nevadensis)

Used primarily in the treatment of venereal disease, the tea was also drunk to stimulate urination.
Poultices were used on wounds.

Indian or Mormon Tea (Univ. Nevada School Med. Collection)

(left) Northern Paiute Shaman, Big Mouth Charlie (Nevada Historical Society) *(below)Big Mouth Charlie's medicine bowl* (Curtis W. Brown Collection)

Nevada Medicine Bottles (Thomas W. Brady Collection)

Dr. Kate Post Van Orden (Stanford
Univ., Lane Med. Lib. Spec. Collection)

Dr. John D. Campbell, Pioche, Nevada
(Courtesy of Linwood Campbell)

Saint Mary Louise Hospital, Virginia City (Nevada Historical Society)

that the Chinese inhabitants of the State had as many doctors, and maybe more, per population as their white neighbors.

[9] Paul D. Duell, "American Frontier Society and Chinese Medicine: The Dimension of an Interaction," Place and Practice: Regional Medicine, Health and Health Care in the Intermountain West, Conference in Reno, Nev., Oct. 22-23, 1993.

[10] David Courtwright, "Opiate Addiction in the American West, 1850-1920" *J. West* XXI, no. 3 (July 1982) pp. 28.

[11] In addition to opium available in Chinese opium dens, raw gum opium, laudanum (tincture of opium), morphine, and patent medicines (Godfrey's Cordial, McMunn's Elixir, and Mrs. Winslow's Soothing Syrup) were readily purchased in pharmacies and other establishments. See Goldman, *Gold Diggers and Silver Miners*, p. 131.

[12] Barlow, *China Doctor of John Day*, pp. 15-16.

CHAPTER FIVE

Civilian Doctors

During the Nevada frontier days, law was in the hands of the people. Survival of the strongest and the power of money prevailed. Furthermore, in the young American democracy, freedom of choice was an important issue. In this environment many cults—Thomsonians, homeopaths, hydropaths, eclectics, and others—flourished and took issue with the conventional practice of medicine. Besides, regular or allopathic doctors were sometimes so unduly severe in their treatment—prescribing mercury to the point of poisoning and bleeding to the point of fainting—that many patients sought alternative treatment. A large number of non-allopathic doctors settled in Nevada during the frontier days, providing an alternative philosophy to conventional medicine. Eclectic physicians comprised the largest group with an alternative philosophy.

Records reveal that eclectic physicians comprised 13.5 per cent (42) of 311 physicians in the state before 1900, while there were 217 regular physicians (69.8 per cent).[1] These figures are derived from the 641 physicians listed in Appendix I. Of these, 311

(48.5 per cent) list either their school of graduation or philosophy of practice. Homeopathic medicine which received much more publicity and currently still has a few proponents, comprised only 7.1 per cent (22 doctors).

The German physician Samuel Hahnemann devised homeopathy in the late 18th century. He based his new medical system on two laws, similars *(similia similibus curantur)*—use of a drug that produces the same symptoms as the disease—and infintestinals—the smaller the dose the better the effect. In fact, drugs were diluted to the point where they had no efficacy. This system appealed to many Americans who were disillusioned with their harsh treatment by regular doctors.[2] Dr. Frederick Hiller, a leading proponent of homeopathy in Virginia City, published two pamphlets on the subject: *Common Sense vs. Allopathic Hum-buggery* and *Medical Truths and Light for the Million*.[3]

In contrast to Hahnemann, Samuel Thomson rebelled against all of the learned professions—law, theology, and medicine. Thomson, a poorly educated New Hampshire farmer who was influenced by Native American herbalists in the Midwest, founded a sectarian group that preached that disease was cold, that treatment consisted of restoring heat and thereby health was regained. In 1806 Thomson began selling his system of instructions and the use of botanical elements, but he left out key ingredients unless the buyer pledged secrecy. For these rights and twenty dollars, the purchaser got the title of doctor.

Thomsonian treatment relied on botanicals, primarily lobelia, an emetic. An example of his healing ritual demonstrates his reliance on herbs.

They started their curing with a steam bath to restore heat, after which a six-step cleansing of the system commenced with emetics, purgatives, enemas, and sweats. The system, based on the use of plants, began with lobelia (pukeweed) mixed with cayenne pepper and brandy to cleanse the stomach, provide heat, and stimulate perspiration. Another steam bath with pepper mixed with ginger prepared the stomach and bowels for scouring with bayberry, rosemary, witch hazel leaves, red raspberry leaves, white pond lily root, the inner bark of hemlock, and the root of marsh rosemary or squaw weed. Next came a dose of bitter plant (either balmony, bitterroot, poplar bark, barberry, or root of goldenseal) to restore digestion. The next step strengthened the bowels by the use of a tonic plant (peach pit meat or cherry stones) mixed with sugar and brandy. The sixth and final step prevented mortification and restored heat by the use of "Rheumatic Drops", wines, brandy, gum myrrh, and cayenne pepper.[4] The motto of the cult was "Puke 'em, sweat 'em, and purge 'em." A favorite recipe was:

To prepare Conserve of Hollyhock.... Take one pound of fresh blossoms; bruise them in a mortar; add four pounds of white sugar; pound them well together until it forms a paste. Then, take the compound of two ounces of poplar bark, two ounces of bayberry, two ounces of nerve powder, one ounce of cayenne, half ounce of bitterroot, mix them well together, and knead it with the pestle in a mortar until it becomes thick as dough. Then, add one table-spoon of the oil of pennyroyal; pound them well together, to be kept in the loaf, rolled into pills. To be taken for all complaints caused by Cold, and other disease, without any regard to names. The above powder, with the same weight of sugar, made fine, will make good spice-bitter for wine. Put two ounces of the compound into one quart. The powders may be eaten dry, or taken in hot water, with more sugar. No spirit is recommended in this medicine.[5]

The Thomsonians appealed to the Mormons who settled Salt Lake City, Genoa (the first settlement in what is now Nevada), and many other communities. The Mormons believed that resorting to a doctor showed lack of faith, but in particular they were suspicious of regular physicians.

On January 3, 1858, Joseph, Brigham Young's elder brother, said, "...I do not believe in doctors; I would rather call upon the Lord." This prejudice against doctors was frequently heard from pulpits in early Utah and Nevada.[6] Even though there were doctors in the Mormon colonies before 1871, few practiced medicine. Thus, the period in which Utah was settled—1847 until 1871 is known as the Premedical Period. Thomsonian doctors held high rank in the church, some being accepted into the priesthood. They referred to the regular doctors as "Poison Doctors."[7]

Before Thomson died in 1843, his leadership was challenged by Alva Curtis who split off and formed the "Literary and Botanico-Medical Institute of Ohio." Further splits led to the establishment of the Eclectics and the Physio-Medicals, and herb doctors, root doctors, and botanics.[8] Eclectic medical schools proliferated and spread across the country. Many botanics, like regular doctors, came to Nevada to seek their fortune. Furthermore, they were accepted by their communities and rose to prominence on the Board of Medical Examiners, the State Board of Health, and the Nevada Medical Society.

Simeon L. Lee, a graduate of the Eclectic Medical College of Cincinnati became the first President of the State Board of Health and the first Secretary of the Board of Medical Examiners. He had a respectable practice in Carson City for many years. His collection of Native American artifacts was donated to the State, and became the Nevada State Museum.

Simeon Bishop, a graduate of the Physio-Medical Institute of Cincinnati, was superintendent of the State Hospital for eight years, and Philippine

Wagner, a homeopathic physician, was on the first Board of Medical Examiners. In the absence of licensing laws, regular doctors found it difficult to oppose these sectarian branches of medicine. On the other hand, many regular doctors were tolerant of them, and some even interacted with them professionally and socially.

All who claimed to be physicians treated the same diseases. In 1862 Richard Francis Burton, the Victorian linguist, explorer, and Orientalist, commented that the most common diseases in the early colonies of what would become Nevada were rheumatism, dysentery, intestinal disorders, and mountain fever.[9] Up through the first quarter of the 20th century, "mountain fever" is frequently noted in patient records. This popular term encompassed most febrile illnesses—including intermittent and remittent fevers (malaria).

Burton also noted eye problems due to dust and glare, respiratory problems such as pneumonia, and dietary problems such as scurvy.[10] "Scurvy when brought in after long desert marches yields to generous diet and vegetables, especially potatoes, which, even in the preserved form, act as a specific."[11]

While in Salt Lake City observing the polygamous practices of the Mormons, Burton noted that "Rheumatism affects the poorer classes, Catarrhs are severe and lasting, Diphtheria is not yet known," and "Measles affects the Indian."[12] He also noted that erysipelas killed many Indians and scrofula (glandular tuberculosis contacted by drinking cow's milk infected with the bovine tuberculosis organism) and phthisis (human tuberculosis of the lungs) were unknown to the white citizens.[13] Burton's observations were not entirely accurate because consumption (phthisis) was frequently listed as the cause of death in early death records.[14]

Just a few years before Burton visited Salt Lake City, a drama with tragic consequence was being played out in Gold Canyon where Gold Hill, Nevada, would be built. In mid August 1857 the Grosh brothers, Hosea Ballou and Ethan Allen, were prospecting when Hosea accidentally struck his foot with his pick. An infection ensued, and despite improvement after poultices of rosin, then bread and soda, a friend was consulted who recommended a poultice of cow dung. Dr. Benjamin L. King agreed that cow dung was the right therapy. The infection progressed and Ethan wrote his father, Rev. A. B. Grosh, requesting money to buy the services of Dr. Charles D. Daggett, the best doctor in the area. Unfortunately, the services of the "best doctor" never came, but Hosea's immortality was established. His treatment, although ill-advised by today's standards, is the first recorded home remedy and medical treatment by a doctor in the Nevada.[15]

Records of military doctors, visitors, and private citizens reflect other diseases that devastated the 19th-century communities in the Great Basin, but the best overview of diseases in a Great Basin mining town is found in the admission records of Saint Mary Louise Hospital in Virginia City.

In 1877 Virginia City was much more sophisticated than other mining camps and early tent cities. The fact that it had a modern hospital meant better health care for its citizens than was generally available throughout the West. Furthermore, its living conditions were better than on the many remote ranches and in the tiny towns that dot the Great Basin. During its first 18 months of operation in 1876-1877, doctors treated 297 patients, who were listed in a large ledger by name, age, occupation, religion, country of birth, admitting diagnosis, and date of admission. These 297 patients represent a cross section of the population and not the total number of those in the community with a certain disease.[16] Also many patients at that time were treated at home.

Fevers of all kinds—intermittent, typhoid, typhus, biliary, stomach, and brain—account for 85 patients or 28.6 percent of the admissions at Saint Mary Louise Hospital. Trauma, an occupational hazard of working in the mines, was second in prominence accounting for 51 patients or nearly 20 percent. Although diarrhea as a cause for admission was given as a diagnosis only 3.4 percent of the time, gastrointestinal complaints, including typhoid fever, were still common, but tapering down from the early days. Rheumatism (rheumatic fever) accounted for 4.4 percent of the admissions. Other diseases—delirium tremens, ophthalmia, syphilis, bronchitis, skin infections, and pleuritis— were relatively minor, but persistent, problems.

Several diseases that were not a problem in military camps in the Great Basin were more common in 1875 Virginia City. These included tuberculosis (6.1 percent), pneumonia (4.7 percent), and psychological diseases such as general and nervous disability which accounted for 7.4 percent of admissions to Saint Mary Louise Hospital. This disorder affected young women who were domestic servants, leading to speculation that the disease was a result of the conditions of employment or the hopelessness of their situation.

Diagnosis and treatment of these conditions generally followed the same lines as in the military hospitals of the Great Basin, but on occasion civilian doctors resorted to the archaic practice of bloodletting. As late as 1892, a physician in Virginia City cupped a half pint of blood from a patient with pneumonia.[17] This practice reflected the hopelessness of the situations and the lack of agreement on the treatment as much as the proven efficacy of the bloodletting. Furthermore, it had been around for centuries and was symbolic for many doctors, but its days were numbered.

The era of bacteriology forever changed the practice of medicine.

---

[1] Foreign graduates are not figured in these statistics unless they also graduated from an American school. Of the 33 foreign graduates two attended both a recognized foreign school and a regular American School.

[2] This refers to the use of mercury and the practice of blood-letting.

[3] The complete titles of Frederick Hiller's treatises are *Common Sense vs. Allopathic Humbuggery; or, Chloroform and Apoplexy Duly Considered in Connection with Certain Allopathic Luminaries* (Virginia, Nev., July 25, 1868); *and Medical Truths and Light for the Million; or, Homeopathy vs. Allopathy* (Virginia, Nev., 1869).

[4] John S. Haller, Jr., *Medical Protestants: The Eclectics in American Medicine, 1825-1939* (Carbondale, Ill.: So. Ill. Univ. Press, 1994) pp. 43-44.

[5] Ralph T., Richards, *Of Medicine, Hospitals, and Doctors* (Salt Lake City: Univ. Utah Press, 1953) p. 14.

[6] *Ibid.*, p. 15.

[7] Joseph R. Morrell, "Medicine of the Pioneer Period in Utah," *Utah Hist Quart.*, XXIII (1955) p.127; John Duffy, "Medicine in the West: an Historical Overview," *J. West* XXI, no. 3 (July 1982) p. 12 and M. R. Walker, *Story of the Nevada State Society and Nevada Medicine* (1937) p. 21.

[8] Allopaths referred to all sectarian doctors, in addition to the eclectics, as irregulars.

[9] Richard F. Burton, *The City of the Saints, and Across the Rocky Mountains to California* (NY: Harper Brothers, 1862) p. 279.

[10] The eye problem that Burton described was most likely trachoma, a disease due to a microscopic organism.

[11] Burton, *The City of the Saints*, p. 278.

[12] Rheumatism is now known as rheumatic fever, and catarrh is a common cold.

[13] *Ibid.*

[14] Richards, *Of Medicine, Hospitals, and Doctors*, pp. 20-21.

[15] Ethan Grosh, Letter to his father, Rev. A. B. Grosh, on September 7, 1857. See Appendix VI for description of the medical treatment and death of Hosea Grosh. Permission to use the letter was granted by Charles T. Wegman of Bloomfield, New Jersey, owner of the letter and a relative of the Grosh Brothers.

[16] St. Mary Louise Hospital Admission Records, Virginia City, Nev.

[17] *The Journals of Alfred Doten*, p. 1831.

CHAPTER SIX

Women Doctors

Between 1851 and 1900, at least 641 civilian physicians of all kinds, as listed in various sources, came to Nevada. Twenty two (3.4 percent) were women. Demographic data is not available on the number or types of patients they saw, although it was common practice for early female physicians to limit their practice to female and pediatric patients.

Records from the Comstock indicate that the first female doctor in 1865, "Doctress Hoffman," treated only children and females.[1] The idea of women becoming physicians was not uniformly accepted in this country, and their professional opportunities were severely restricted. In fact, in 1848 the first woman graduate of an American medical school, Elizabeth Blackwell, was ostracized by the other lodgers at her eastern boarding house. However, the opposition slowly crumbled. By 1870 there were 525 women physicians in the United States.[2] And, there was less opposition to them in the West, where there was greater need and medical tradition was less established.

Even so, barriers existed in the West for female medical students. Cooper Medical School (now

Stanford University Medical School), founded in
1858, didn't graduate its first woman physician until
1877; Toland Medical College (now the University
of California at San Francisco) graduated its first
woman the following year in 1878. However, as late
as 1894 women had to struggle to gain recognition
from their fellow students. Nellie Doyle described
her efforts at Toland Medical College in *Doctor Nellie.* In fact, the dean showed his bias when he
changed her name to Helen because he felt the
name of Nellie was not dignified. After graduation
in 1894, Dr. Doyle returned to the Owens Valley to
practice, eventually marrying Doctor McKnight, a
graduate of Rush Medical College, who came west
to run the Wild Rose Mine.[3]

Between the 1870s and 1900 at least 13 percent of
Stanford's graduates and 10 percent of California's
were women.[4] In spite of the number of female
graduates available in neighboring California, less
than four percent of the physicians in Nevada at
that time were female. There are many reasons for
this disparity. First, the mining camps of the Great
Basin were overwhelmingly male, leaving little
opportunity for an individual who treated primarily women and children. Second, conditions were
primitive and not as desirable for establishing a
new practice as in larger cities. Furthermore, it was
difficult for a woman physician to move to a raw

mining town and establish a practice unless she was married or her family lived in the community.

This story of women physicians in 19th-century Nevada reflected the prejudices of the rest of the country, but they were a vital source of medical care.

---

[1] There is some indication that Doctress Hoffman performed abortions. Her advertisement in the *Enterprise* is addressed "To the Ladies" and offers confidential treatment of "female complaints." Marion S. Goldman, *Gold Diggers and Silver Miners* (Ann Arbor: Univ. Mich. Press, 1981) p. 127.

[2] William Forrest Sprague, *Women and the West A Short Social History* (Boston: Christopher Pub. House, 1940) p. 139.

[3] See Mary Austin, foreword, *Doctor Nellie* (Mammoth Lakes, Calif.: Genny Smith Books, 1983).

[4] These statistics are derived from the directories of graduates where sex is not indicated. Many names are initials only and can assumed to be males. A female designation is assigned if the given name is feminine.

CHAPTER SEVEN

Early Midwives
by Phyllis Cudek

A history of medicine in Nevada would not be complete without noting the presence and contributions of midwives. Distances between settlements and scarcity of physicians coupled with a tradition of women assisting women during childbirth accounts for the importance of midwives in the West.[1]

The wagon trains bearing pioneers included pregnant women and midwives who could attend to them during childbirth. Isolated communities through which the wagon trains passed also had a need for the knowledge and experience brought by midwives. Outbreaks of smallpox, influenza, and other such illnesses required as much medical assistance as could be found in the area, and midwives were often the only persons available with any medical experience. Their knowledge of home remedies and use of herbal ingredients was often invaluable to the settlers' health. So scarce were medical supplies that cactus fiber was occasionally used to suture wounds.[2]

Although the importance of midwives was undeniable, they rarely listed themselves as "professionals" in county census reports or city directories. For example, in *Bishop's Directory of Virginia City, Gold Hill, Silver City, Carson City, and Reno, 1878-79*, professions such as dressmakers, milliners, domestics, teachers, and ladies' nurses were listed; however, only two midwives, a Mrs. Julia Bellmere of Virginia City and Mrs. S. M. Drannan of Reno, were acknowledged in addition to Mrs. Helen Anderson of Reno, who was listed as midwife and physician. Midwives were crucial to the sustained population growth of rural communities. They enabled the West to grow and prosper because of their maternal and childbirth attention and skills.

The Church of Latter Day Saints (Mormons) contributed widely to the presence and importance of midwifery in Nevada in the 19th and early 20th centuries. Settlements established under the direction of the Mormon Church in Salt Lake City took families to remote areas of the state. The proliferation of children demonstrated the need for childbirth assistance; therefore, women were often chosen from their communities to travel to Salt Lake City to be trained in the techniques of midwifery and who then would return to their communities to practice.

In 1891 Panaca in southeastern Nevada was such a community. One of its midwives was Mariah Berdilla Rich (née Atchison). This woman delivered Nevada W. Driggs, who later wrote an article for Nevada Historical Quarterly describing childbirth in a small western town.[3] Two other women from the Mormon Church, well known in their community of White Pine County were Mrs. Mary Leicht Oxborrow and Mrs. Margaret Christina Arnoldus Windous.

Author Effie Oxborrow Read writes about midwives, Mary Leicht Oxborrow (her grandmother), and Margaret Christina Arnoldus Windous, in *White Pine Lang Syne, A True History of White Pine County, Nevada.*

In 1900 Mrs. Mary Leicht Oxborrow came from St. George, Utah.

She had been set aside by the Church authorities as a midwife and doctor for the community of Lund. She already had sons and daughters there. Her excellence as a Doctor cannot be over-commended. She made her own medicines, salves, face cream, and had keen knowledge of herbs. She accomplished tremendous medical feats in care of broken bones and cuts. She delivered 235 babies, two of whom were her own great grandchildren. She was an excellent musician and was a beloved character.[4]

Read continues later in her book with information on another much admired midwife and doctor, Margaret Christina Arnoldus Windous.

> In 1908 the Latter Day Saints Church requested that each ward of the Church send at least one Relief Society member to Salt Lake City to train under the direction of Mrs. (Dr.) Ramona B. Pratt. Mrs. Windous had eight children and limited education, but she accomplished this mission and received certification for practicing obstetrics and nursing. She was the country doctor, and it was necessary for her to make many lonely trips across the desert in the dead of night with her little black buggy and faithful horse, Dolly.[5]

Mrs. Windous lived in Nevada from 1899, had a Maternity Home in Lund, and delivered more than 1,000 babies. Her patients were of all nationalities and religions, writes Read.

Most communities had their own midwife who could be summoned for an expected birth. Midwives, unlike physicians, gave family assistance in ways other than delivering a child. A midwife would leave her own family while she gave physical and emotional support to the expectant woman, often cooking meals, doing laundry and housecleaning, and caring for other family members after the birth of a new baby. This service would often last several days before and/or after the childbirth;

on the frontier women helped women in any way possible.

In Nevada's early days it was not unusual for a mother to be a midwife to her daughter, daughter-in-law, her granddaughter, or for a sister to be a midwife to her own sister. Although a midwife was usually a woman who had given birth to children herself, it was not uncommon for a young girl to assist a family member in the birthing process, thereby providing her with experience to assist others as she grew older.

A few illustrations of midwifery activities follow. Anna Mueller Engel Neddenriep was a German immigrant and qualified midwife who wore a long black cape as a symbol of her profession. She was often referred to as an "angel of mercy" by her Carson Valley neighbors.[6] Around 1900 Mrs. Mary "Granny" Dakin offered "hospital" services in Elko after having been a midwife for many years and also having taught midwifery to her daughter, Mrs. Tillie Roach (Mrs. Amos Roach).[7] Mrs. Bill Bradley, a midwife for the White Pine County area was "untutored," but would "often...tie her own small baby to her back Indian-style, saddle a pony, and ride twenty miles or more to be on hand for the blessed event."[8] A Mrs. Scott from Osceola was midwife for Anna Day Swallow in the Shoshone area around the 1880s. Despite her lack of formal medical training "Little Mrs. Dr. Swallow" cared for burns, pneumonia, and delivered babies in her community. She would often travel in the dead of night by horse and sleigh in two feet of snow to reach a patient.[9] There are certainly hundreds of untold similar incidences of the unselfishness and devotion displayed by 19th-century women in the vast state of Nevada.

The treatment given by midwives was usually non-interventionist. Although forceps had been used for hundreds of years, and were sometimes present in the "medical bag" of a midwife, they were often reserved for use by a physician for a difficult delivery. Administration of ergot, a commercially prepared medicine formulated from a rye grain fungus, was used by midwives and physicians to produce contractions of the uterus and curtail postpartum bleeding. Other home remedies known by particular midwives were no doubt used to provide comfort, but generally childbirth was accomplished on the frontier without aid or medication.

Puerperal fever, commonly known as childbed fever, was a constant threat to the life of a delivering mother. However, once the importance of cleanliness and sterilization became known, this condition became less prevalent. As Nevada's population grew, some of the larger communities, such as Elko, Ely, and Reno had maternity homes or hospitals, which were usually operated by nurses or midwives. Some women would come for the birth of a child and then remain for several days to heal and regain strength before returning home to their families.

Because of the anonymity of many midwives in Nevada's wide open spaces, finding and documenting names of women who aided other women, and also performed many medical services for their communities, is difficult and many times impossible. Terminology in reference to midwives adds frustration to research efforts; midwives may also be referred to as ladies' nurses or Doctresses which could also refer to female physicians, or merely those who treat sick or injured people. Also present were a few men who signed birth certificates as "accoucheur," which can be interpreted as a male midwife or an obstetrician, but not necessarily a physician. The moral atmosphere of the 1800s and early 1900s contributed to the obscurity of midwife identification in that "genteel" women did not discuss birthing nor intimate personal life in general.

However, upon surveying the 1880 U.S. Census, only three "ladies' nurses" were listed in population reports for the counties of White Pine, Eureka, Lander, Elko, and Lincoln. When a community numbered over one thousand people, as Eureka County did in 1880, it must be assumed that there were quite a few undeclared midwives giving assistance during birth and providing medical services when required.

United States births, by 1900, were assisted approximately equally by both midwives and physicians.[10] This was not true in the sparsely populated state of Nevada. The early female settlers of the state were immigrants who were carrying on family traditions for birthing or who may have learned their professions from other experienced women. Most were not formally trained unless they had acquired skills in schools in northern or western Europe. Their chosen obligation to midwifery extended from birth to death. Included in their practice was preparation of the body for burial.

All phases of the immigrants' lives were touched by the community midwife.[11]

[1] Nevada State law, beginning in 1882, required that all births be recorded by the county recorder, however the law was not always observed or enforced. The State subsequently tightened the law and required certification of birth beginning on July 1, 1911.

[2] Bobette Perrone, H. Henrietta Stockel, and Victoria Krueger, *Medicine Women, Curranderas, and Women Doctors* (Norman, Okla.: Univ. Okla. Press, 1989) p.128.

[3] Driggs, Nevada W., "How Come Nevada," *Nev. Hist. Soc. Quart.* XIV, no. 3 (Fall 1973) pp. 184-185.

[4] Effie O. Read, *White Pine Lang Syne: A True* History *of White Pine County, Nevada* (Denver: Big Mountain Press, 1965) p. 64.

[5] *Ibid.,* p. 80.

[6] Marion Ellison, "Angel of Mercy," Stanley W. Paher, ed., *Nevada Towns and Tales, Vol. 1* (Las Vegas, Nev.: Nevada Pub., 1981-1982) p. 56.

[7] Patterson, *Sagebrush Doctors,* p. 97.

[8] Read. *White Pine Lang Syne.* p. 210.

[9] *Ibid.,* p.182.

[10] Judith Walzer Leavitt, *Brought to Bed: Childbearing in America, 1750-1950* (NY: Oxford Univ. Press, 1986) p. 267.

[11] There were probably several Chinese midwives in 19th-century Nevada since midwifery was an old and important practice in China. Sue F. Chung interviewed the daughter of Mrs. Chow Sing Huey, a Chinese midwife in turn of the century

Carson City who also administered to the Paiute community and fluently spoke their language.

CHAPTER EIGHT

Home Remedies

Many cultural groups rely on the use of home remedies rather than treatment by a doctor. Consultation with family or friends for advice on medical problems is a natural process. Since acquaintances might have had similar problems that yielded to practical and accessible remedies, their advice was sought and followed. In the Great Basin, travelers, ranchers, miners, and settlers followed this simple natural process. In fact, today, we would consider much of what the educated civilian doctor practiced in the 19th century to be little more than application of home remedies. In Austin, Nevada, Dr. Riddle in 1868 treated typhoid fever with mustard baths and brandy rubs, an acknowledged Basque home remedy.[1] It is reasonable to assume that if someone else in the family showed symptoms similar to those of typhoid fever, they were treated in the same manner without contacting Dr. Riddle.

Furthermore, in a setting such as the Great Basin, professional medical care was frequently days away, in one of five or six populated areas. Due to the sparse population in the 19th-century West and in many other parts of the United States the philosophy of self help was prevalent to a much greater extent than it has been in the 20th century. Even today in remote areas of the Great Basin it is still necessary to rely on home remedies before professional help can be obtained. Unfortunately, some sick people also could not afford to pay for medical care and had to rely solely on home treatment. In actuality, most 19th-century doctors accepted free care as a way of life. Other patients would not seek medical care from a doctor because of religious belief.

When doctors were not available, the first white travelers in the Great Basin had to rely on their medicine chest or on help from other members of the party. These emigrants carried various medicinal compounds in their baggage. Narcotics—morphine, laudanum, opium, or Dover's powders— were used for sedation, analgesia and to treat diarrhea. A second important group included purging agents; calomel (mercurous chloride) was administered for a number of ailments. Similarly, cream of tartar with antimony, Epsom salts, and castor oil were used as emetics. A third important group comprised the alcohol solutions which were considered to be stimulants. Alcohol was an important ingredient of patent medicines. Brandy, whiskey, and other spirits were used internally and externally. Also carried with the wagon trains were camphor, flaxseed oil, ginger, horehound, ammonia, carbolic acid, hartshorn, quinine, sulphur, turpentine, and many other herbs and chemical compounds. If the concoctions were not palatable, molasses, honey, sugar or other sweeteners were added as sweeteners.[2]

When Raymond Doetsch crossed the Great Basin in a wagon, he described the medicine chest as containing "Elixirs, tonics, salves, balms, unctions, and ointments, together with 'physiking pills', laudanum, calomel [mercurous chloride], essence of peppermint, castor oil, and a few patent medicines."[3]

Just as important as available medicine were the various health care guide books that promulgated the various treatments and philosophies of medicine in the 19th century. In 1769 William Buchan wrote and published the first self help book, *Domestic Medicine*, in Edinburgh, Scotland. Written to educate and inform the public on the prevention of disease, it appeared in America approximately 100 years later, and became popular. Buchan's book was written for the "rural elite" to treat their neighbors. It contained descriptions of the diseases and their symptoms, followed by their treatment.[4]

Many other books were published in America, but probably the most important was John C. Gunn's *Domestic Medicine, or Poor Man's Friend*, first published in 1830. Gunn, an educated

physician, taught that every aspect of medicine
could be practiced by the common man when the
practice of medicine was reduced "to principles of
common sense." He directed his treatise "for families of Western and Southern States."[5] Doten
described his reliance on Gunn:

> July 1 [1850]...Eunice prepared, and I took the
> following simple remedy, from "Gunn's Domes-
> tic Medicine"—for ague and fever—Make a
> good sized cup of strong Coffee, sweeten it well,
> and mix it with an equal quantity of lime or
> lemon juice—The dose to be taken just before
> the shake is expected and must be taken warm
> and on an empty stomach...
> July 2—Today in spite of the coffee remedy I
> had a strong touch of the ague & fever, and a
> pretty tough time of it...
> July 3—This morning I took one of Bennett's
> powders and had no signs of ague or fever all
> day...[6]

Home remedies were not without side effects, and
Doten describes, "My back along the spine is all blis-
tered and sore from the mustard plaster I have
applied lately—."[7] In the self-reliance atmosphere
of the 19th century some authors went beyond
mustard plaster and drug treatment by stating that
any man could perform surgical operations such as
amputations.

In addition to self-help books, many sects and
ethnic groups relied on remedies indigenous to
their culture. Latter Day Saints (Mormons) settled

wide areas of the Great Basin before and during the mining explorations, while the Basques came later with the growing sheep industry. Both of these groups had home remedies passed down by their elders.

A typical old world Basque remedy consisted of a mixture of dried mustard and wood ashes added to hot water for soaking feet to ward off a cold. Whiskey, kerosene and lard plasters was also topically applied to the chest for colds.[8] Also kerosene and chicken fat were rubbed on the chest to relieve cold symptoms.[9] Sore throats were treated by drinking hot water with ashes and crushed mustard.[10] Another remedy was the use of hot water, whiskey, and lemon juice to relieve the symptoms of fever and the common cold.[11]

A Basque remedy for an earache involved plugging the ear with a cotton pledget after blowing smoke into the ear canal. Warm cooking oil was sometimes used in the ear instead of smoke.[12] Another oil, castor oil was ingested for stomach aches, and was used to cleanse the bowel and alleviate constipation.[13]

Garlic was used widely in Basque culture. Internally, garlic soup was given to alleviate the symptoms of the common cold, and externally, garlic cloves were bound to wounds to promote healing.[14] Garlic and vegetable oil were applied to boils, and the patient drank the purulent material extracted from the boil to effect a cure. Garlic was sautéed in olive oil until the garlic was a golden color. A cloth soaked in the oil was wrapped around a sore or the infected part.[15] Onions also were used in a similar fashion. One half of a raw yellow onion was applied to an infected part to bring the infection to a head.[16]

Other plant products were used to effect a cure. The outer hull of a walnut was boiled in water. The vapor was inhaled for colds. Extremities were held over the steam vapor and wrapped in a wool cloth. Sometimes a cloth was soaked in the solution and applied to a joint or sore extremity.[17]

Poultices were made by placing bread dough in a towel or sock, and wrapping it around the afflicted area or sore throat from a cold.[18] Some families used oatmeal in a similar manner to relieve a sore throat.[19] Others treated the cough due to a cold with a "disgusting tasting tea" made from boiled cherry tree bark.[20]

Many Basques used superstition and magic to cure conditions such as warts. To effect the cure a potato was cut into four pieces to simulate a cross, rubbed on the wart, and buried in the ground in a manner reminiscent of Native American practices. Another treatment consisted of rubbing the blood from the cock's comb of a freshly killed rooster on a wart and burying the comb in a secret place by the side of the road. The wart was magically transmitted to the next person who passed by.[21]

Basque immigrants in the Great Basin were experts in animal husbandry. Some of the therapy used for animals was used on family members. Horse liniment was rubbed on the skin to relieve pain and soreness.[22] Animal products were also used. Cow manure was used on burns, as were some local plants.[23] Urine had wide use in Mormon folklore. It was used to treat chapped skin, sore eyes, earache, and was given internally to babies with the croup. Baby urine was also applied to normal skin to improve the complexion.[24]

In addition to the use of excreta, pioneer Mormon home remedies also included the use of animals and animal parts. Brains were rubbed on the gums of a child perceived to be suffering from teething. Chicken liver was rubbed on a wart, and the liver was then buried in the ground. Live animals were also used to treat serious and life threatening illness. Live chickens or pigeons were split open and applied to the chest as a poultice to treat pneumonia or applied to the neck for treatment of diphtheria.[25]

More important to Mormon tradition was the use of herbs, sagebrush, and the divinely inspired "Brigham tea." Widely used throughout the Great Basin, Brigham tea is made from several plants, but the most important ingredient was a septated reed-like grass known as *Ephedra viderens* or *E. Nevadensis* that contains a mild stimulant, ephedrine. Tea made from this plant and the common sagebrush were not only drank, but they were also used topically on sores, sprains and in poultices. They were used as stimulants and tonics in the spring to purify the blood. Women used sagebrush tea to wash, invigorate, and rejuvenate their hair.[26]

No discussion of home remedies is complete without reviewing some of the patent medicines and the accompanying medicine shows that visited the Great Basin. These shows not only promoted patent medicines with their all-healing powers, but they provided entertainment when a vaudeville to the remote mining camps.

In Virginia City in 1891, Doten described the Pawnee Medicine Doctor Troupe with its month-long entertainment which was free except for Thursday night and Saturday, when the show cost 25¢. There was a variety of performers, "in varieties, song, dance, juggling, acrobatic." The two doctors with the show provided consultations and sold bushels of "Too-re, Pain Balm, Magic Salve, Worm Destroyer, etc."

In 1895 Vivian DeMonto's Superb Company came to Virginia City with a "Big tent show... dramatic, variety, song, dance, aerobatic, medicine selling, etc.—15 cts admission." There were also street medicine shows, such as the Quaker Doctors, and shows at the Opera House, such as the Kickappoo

Vaudeville and Medicine Show. Another street show had three fakirs in a wagon with banjo, an organ and a "great talker" selling Franklin Oil, a wonderful pain killer.[27]

Doten was not the only chronicler of medicine shows on the Nevada frontier. Dan De Quille described the sale of quack nostrums, electrical machines, and an "apparatus for testing the strength of the lungs, and a thousand other similar thing." He writes:

> Who is the next gentleman who wishes to try the battery? It makes the old man feel young, and the young man feel strong. Remember, gentlemen, that a quarter of a dollar pays the bill....Purifies the blood, strengthens the nervous system; cures headaches, toothaches, neuralgia, and all diseases of the nervous system....Try the battery! Try the battery![28]

Besides machines that increased the quality of life, an astounding variety of medicines that cured all diseases were hawked by traveling medicine shows, quacks, physicians, drugstores, and anyone else who wanted to "make a buck." Dr. J. A. Huntsman of Battle Mountain sold Extract of Alba Salvia for beautifying and restoring the hair. Dr. Louis Terry in Elko sold Nevada's White Sage Natural Hair Restorative, and Dr. J. J. McBride sold King of Pain tonic.[29] Dr. A. T. McMurtrey sold his cure-all in Virginia City, Nevada, and Radway's

Sarsaparilian Resolvent was available to cure ovarian tumors. Dr. Walker's Vinegar Bitters cured all female complaints. Even testimonials in the local papers praised the miracle medicines and their healing powers.[30]

Local papers, including *The Territorial Enterprise*, advertised remedies to treat venereal disease. Red Drops, Unfortunate's Friend, Pine Knot Bitters, and others were sold in liquor stores and pharmacies. Local doctors also advertised "Infallible Remedies" and dishonestly promised cures for "private diseases."[31] When these measures failed Dr. Hiller was present with his unfailing knives to cut off the offending part. Doten records, "Cut off about 2 inches of his penis—the head all rotten with the pox."[32]

This brief overview of the self-remedies available on the Great Basin during the frontier days provides a glimpse at society and its search for a cure of its diseases. As medical diagnosis and treatment became more scientific, people relied less on quackery and magical cures.

However, quackery is not dead today, and in hopeless, incurable—and even not so hopeless—conditions, people still search for a miraculous, unscientific cure.

[1] Marvin, Lewis, *Martha and the Doctor: A Frontier Family in Central Nevada* (Reno: Univ. Nev. Press, 1977) p. 188.

[2] Austin E. Fife, "Pioneer Mormon Remedies," *Western Folklore* 16 no. 3 (1957) pp. 153-154. Patent medicines sometimes contained some form of narcotic.

[3] Raymond N. Doetsch, *Journey to the Green and Golden Lands: The Epic of Survival on the Wagon Trail* (Port Washington, NY.: National Univ. Pub., 1976) p. 42.

[4] Charles E. Rosenberg, "Medical Text and Social Context: Explaining William Buchan's *Domestic Medicine*," *Bull. Hist. Med.* 57 (1983) pp. 24-25.

[5] Charles S. Rosenberg, *Explaining Epidemics and Other Studies* (NY: Cambridge Univ. Press, 1992) pp. 57 and 62. For a more complete discussion of the topic see Guenter B. Risse, Ronald L. Numbers and Judith Walzer Leavitt ed., *Medicine without Doctors: Home Health Care in American History* (NY: Science Hist. Pub., 1977) and John Duffy, "Medicine in the West: An Historical Overview," *J. West* XXI, no. 3 (July 1982).

[6] *The Journals of Alfred Doten*, p. 73.

[7] *Ibid.* p 259.

[8] Sarah Catherine Baker, "Basque American Folklore in Eastern Oregon," Berkeley, Univ. Calif., M.A. Thesis, 1972, pp. 128-131.

[9] Basque remedy related by John Legarza, Reno, Nevada, to the author.

[10] Sarah Baker, "Basque American Folklore in Eastern Oregon," pp. 128-131.

[11] Basque remedy related by John Legarza.

---

[12] Linda Dufurenna, "Pete Bengochea Oral History," Winnemucca, 1993-94, p.173.

[13] Basque remedy related by John Legarza.

[14] *Ibid.*, p. 130. Also Linda Dufurenna, "Marguerite Dufurenna Stephens Oral History," Winnemucca, 1994, tape 11.

[15] Basque remedy related by Leon Urrutia, Los Banos, to Noeline Etchegoyhen Bross.

[16] *Ibid.*

[17] *Ibid.*

[18] Dufurenna, "Bengochea Oral History," p.173.

[19] Basque remedy related by John Legarza.

[20] Basque remedy related by Noeline Etchegoyhen Bross, Portola, California, to the author.

[21] Basque remedy related by Leon Urrutia.

[22] Basque remedy related by John Legarza.

[23] Dufurenna, "Bengochea Oral History," p.130.

[24] Fife, "Pioneer Mormon Remedies," p. 156.

[25] *Ibid.* , p. 157 and Sohn, "Sylvain Oral History."

[26] Fife, "Pioneer Mormon Remedies," pp. 155-156.

[27] *The Journals of Alfred Doten*, pp. 1637-2130 passim.

[28] Dan De Quille (William Wright), *The Big Bonanza: An Authentic Account of the Discovery,, History, and Working of the World-Renowned Comstock Lode of Nevada...* (NY: Alfred A., 1953), p. 297.

[29] Patterson, *Sagebrush Doctors*, pp. 69-70.

[30] Barbara Cloud, "Images of Women in the Mining-Camp Press," *Nev. Hist. Soc. Quart.* 36, no. 3 (Fall 1993) p. 205. For a more complete description of patent medicine see James Harvey Young, *The Toadstool Millionaires: A Social History of Patent*

Medicines in America before Federal Regulation (Princeton: Princeton Univ. Press, 1961).

[31] Goldman, *Gold Diggers and Silver Miners*, p. 131.

[32] *The Journals of Alfred Doten*, p. 897.

19th-Century Medical Doctors[1]

Name	Source	Location & Date	Born/Education
Adams, H. S.	7, 30.	Carson City '77, EC '79.	Unk/Mo Med Coll.
Adams, W. F.	40.	WC '74.	Unk/Miss Med Coll.
Aiken, Perley J.	4, 23, 6k, 6l, 6m, 6n, 3.	Virginia City '75-'81.	Ohio/Jefferson Med Coll.
Aitchison, George	1, 9, 6e, 6b, 6c, 6j, 6i, 6k, 6l, 6m, 6n, 6o, 21, 2, 39, 63.	Virginia City '63-'81.	Scotland/Unk.
Ajlen, O. S.	6c.	Virginia City '64.	Unk.
Alban, William G.	24, 6a.	Gold Hill, SC '61-'63, Attend Nev Constit Convent.	Ohio/Unk.
Albers, Annet	43. No records at BME, maybe did not practice med.[2]	WC '00.	Germany/Unk.
Alexander, G. R.	18, 68.	Nev pre '65, Pioche, LC '81.	Unk.
Allen, George P.	40.	WC '84.	Unk/U Mich.
Allen, T. C.	21, 25, 6e, 8, 6j.	Utah Terr '60, Carson City '73-'74.	Unk.
Ambroseuf, Silvestro Ambrosio (S. A. Ambrose)	30, 9.	Carson City '96.	Unk/U St Petersburg, Russia (Fraudulent according to Doten).
Andersen, Helen	6m, 3.	Reno '78-'79, Carson City '80.	Denmark/Unk.

Name	Refs	Location	School
Anderson, A.	6n.	Gold Hill, SC '80-'81.	Unk.
Anderson, Charles Lewis	6b, 4, 74 (picture), 75, 76.	Carson City '62-'67, 1st Nev Surg Gen, Supt Schools OC, 1st Nev botanist, Santa Cruz, Calif '67, Died '10.	Va/ Asbury (Depauw) Coll, Ind.
Anderson, J. Elwood	23, 30, 40.	Carson City, WC, Virginia City '87.	Unk/Pulte Med Coll,Cincinnati. (Homeo).
Anthony, Jesse Cram	4, 23.	Virginia City '96, Died SF, Calif.	Maine/Bellevue Hosp Med Coll.
Asher, John Alfred	8, 21, 41, 43, 64.	Carson City '98, Cherry Ck, ElC '00, Sparks '03, Co phy '06, Sparks Health Officer '08, St Senator '08.	Ill/Coll Phy Surg Chicago.
Atwater, Hattie F.	4, 30.	Carson City '82.	Unk/Wooster Med Coll, Cleveland.
Bacon, E, M,	6b.	Aurora, EC '63.	Unk.
Baiodux, (Mayer?)	43, No records at BME.	Carson City '00.	At sea, parents from Germany /Unk.
Banks, Frederick X. (T. C?)	2, 21, 4, 24, 6n, 60, 15, 43, 63, 64.	Unionville, HC '65-'81, Lovelock, HC '00, Reno '99.	La/Med Coll La.
Barker, D. H.	6n.	Reno '81.	Unk.
Barnes, Thomas L.	6c.	Gold Hill, SC '64.	Unk.
Barrett, William	40.	WC '81.	Unk/Wisc Med Coll.
Barrette, H. S.	24.	Susanville (Calif), Utah Terr '60.	Unk.
Bateman, Alex	2, 21.	ElC '70.	Tenn/Unk.

Name		Location	School
Bazet, Louis (Ludorico)	30, 26, 61.	Eureka, EuC, '76-'78, Calif St Bd of Health.	Unk/Jefferson Med Coll.
Bazon, Dr.	8.	Eureka, EuC, '75.	Unk.
Bean, James Arandel	4, 21, 6f, 18, 3, 24.	Battle Mtn, LaC '79-'80, Eureka, EuC, & NC '81.	NH/Art Medics, (Williamette U Med Dept) Salem, Oreg.
Bean, Joseph Allen	27.	Battle Mtn, LaC '80.	Unk/U Mich.
Bell, J. N.	16, 4.	Winnemucca, HC '71.	Unk/Art Medics, (Williamette U Med Dept) Salem, Oreg.
Bell, Rezin	1, 21, 24, 6a, 2, 39, 8, 61, 6o.	Virginia City '60, Pyr Lake War '60,Hamilton, WPC '70-'77.	Va/Transylvania Med Coll, Lexington, Ky.
Bench, Alfred K.	3.	Elko '80.	NY/Unk.
Benny, J. L.	40.	WC '92.	Unk/Med U Phila.
Bergman, C. H.	61.	Winnemucca, HC '78.	Unk.
Bergman, William S.	2, 21, 6f, 6g, 6h, 6j, 6i, 6l, 6m, 6n, 6o, 63, 19 (11.23.70).	Reno '70-'81.	Germany/Unk.
Bergstein, Henry	20, 8, 21, 23, 25, 6f, 24, 6k, 6l, 6m, 9, 64, 65, 43, 59, 41 (picture), 68, 84.	Pioche, LC '72-'74 , Supt St Hosp '95-'98, Virginia City '75-'79, Nev Assemb '75, Pres NSMS '94, Reno '95-'00, Died SF, Calif.	Germany/ Cooper Med Coll.
Berkstein, H.	63.	SC '75.	Va/Unk.
Berthier, Alfred	6c, 6g, 6h, 6j, 6p, 6o, 2.	Virginia City '64-'74, SC Phy '73-'74.	Germany/Unk.
Betzel, C. W.	6k.	Virginia City '77.	Unk.

Bien, H. M.	24, 84.	Nev Assemb '64, SC '62, Virginia City '64, Ed Nevada Staats Zeitung.	Unk.
Bird, Nelson John	4, 6p.	Virginia City '67, Died Fresno, Calif '04.	Unk/Queens U Fac Med, Royal Coll Phy Surg.
Bishop, Alva C.	4, 8, 21, 25, 24, 6g, 6h, 6l, 6n, 6o, 26, 39, 3, 63, 65, 68. (Bro of Simeon)	Nev '69, Wadsworth, WC '71, Pioche, LC '72- '74, Eureka, EuC '74-'81, Austin, LaC, Wadsworth '72.	Ill/Eclectic Med Coll Cincinnati.
Bishop, Simeon	4, 21, 25, 6l, 6e, 8, 6c, 6j, 6i, 6m, 6n, 6p, 6o, 2, 39, 3, 19 (11.23.70), 58, 63, 65.	Gold Hill, SC '64, Huffakers, WC '67, WC '68-'69, Reno '70-'81, SC '70, Supt St Hosp '83-'91.	Pa (Ohio?)/ Physio-Med Inst Cincinnati (Eclectic).
Bishop, Willard J.	4, 21, 39, 63.	NC '75, Wadsworth, WC '77.	Vt/Eclectic Med Coll Cincinnati.
Bjornson, A.	68.	Pioche, LC '94.	Unk.
Black, E. D.	8, 21, 2, 10, 24, 6l, 6o, 48 (5.20.77), 49 (10.27.80), 63.	Genoa, DC '64- '83, DC Trea, DC Phy '83.	Ohio/Unk.
Blackwood, Char- les W.	6n.	Paradise, HC '80-'81.	Unk.
Blackwood, T. F	23, 6k, 6l.	Virginia City '76, Silver City, LyC '77-'78.	Unk/Jefferson Med Coll.
Boatman, Nathan C.	6o, 39, 4.	Mtn City, ElC '71-'71, Mtn City '77, Died Wash '82.	Unk/Med Coll Ohio, Cincinnati Med Coll.
Bogman, Charles H.	22, 21, 6l, 38, 63.	Winnemucca, HC '75-'78.	RI/Jefferson Med Coll.
Bonham, B. B.	25, 8, 6b.	WC '60s.	Unk.
Borrette, A. G. (H. S.)	3, 6n.	Elko '80.	England/Unk.
Bowling, C.	6n.	McDermit, HC '80.	Unk.

Braman, Jason J.	4, 30, 6l, 6m.	Carson City '75-'79.	Unk/Toland Med Coll.
Brenson, W. S.	63.	SC '75.	NY/Unk.
Brierly, Conant Bowin	24, 6n.	Sutro, LyC '80-'81, US Army '69-'74.	Unk/Cooper Med Coll.
Bright, J. J.	63.	SC '75.	NY/Unk.
Bronson, Abraham	6o.	Golconda, HC '71-'72.	Unk.
Bronson, William S.	22, 21, 8, 6e, 6j, 6f, 9, 6g, 32, 6m, 6n, 6p, 6o, 39, 3, 29 (9.22.75).	Virginia City '65-'87, Winnemucca, HC '75.	NY/Unk.
Brooks, Dr.	2, 21.	Unionville, HC '70.	OH/Unk.
Brower, H.S.	6j.	Reno '74.	Unk.
Brown, David P.	21, 6e, 6g, 6p, 6o.	Virginia City '67, '72.	Unk.
Brown, Marshall Augustus	23, 4.	Virginia City '79, Died Marshall, Mo.	Unk/Calif Med Assoc, SF, Calif (Eclectic).
Bruck, Alex	23.	Virginia City '75.	Unk/Friedrick Wilhelm Inst, Königsberg.
Bryant, Edmund Gardner	23, 24, 17, 5, 6b, 8, 60.	Virginia City, Pyr Lake War '60, Steamboat Springs, WC '63, Died La Porte, Calif 6.20.66.	Unk/Coll Phy Surg NY
Bryarly, Wakeman	62, 9, 6p, 6c, 61.	Virginia City '61, Died Md '69.	Md/Wash Med Coll Balto.
Buchins, A. C. (Doctress)	21, 63.	Elko '75.	La/Unk.
Buncher, W.	9, 6j.	Dayton, LyC '72-'74.	Unk /Supt Rock Pt Mill, Dayton.
Burbank, Dr.	9.	Virginia City '63.	Unk.
Burgi, Peter	4, 6k, 6l, 6m, 6n, 3.	Silver City, LyC '77-'81.	Switzerland/ Jefferson Med Coll.

Burnsey, J.	63.	SC '75.	Tenn/Unk.
Busay, Bennett	11.	Elko '76.	Unk/U Md.
Callahan, J. J.	21, 6l, 6n, 6o, 2.	Wapias, LC '70, Carlin, ElC '71-'72, NC '78-'81.	NY/Unk.
Campbell, John Dalglesh	4, 21, 25, 18, 64, 68, 84, 57.	Cherry Ck, WPC '82, Taylor, WPC '83, Pioche, LC '92, Nev Senate '17-21, Died Salt Lake City '22.	Mich/U Mich.
Campbell, S. D.	6c.	Gold Hill, SC '64.	Unk.
Carpenter, W.	1.	Gold Hill, SC '60.	NY/Unk.
Cavel, Herbert Bertram	4, 30.	Carson City '94.	Unk/Royal Coll Surg England.
Chaigneau, Victor A.	28, 4, 18, 68.	Heney, NC '81, Pioche, LC '92.	Unk/U Calif.
Chamberlin, R . (Phelps)	1, 21, 6a, 50 (12.6.75).	Genoa, DC '60-'75.	Vt/Unk.
Chamberlin, M. A.	23, 26, 40, 39.	Eureka '75-'77, Virginia City '77, WC '79.	Unk/Med Coll St Louis, Mo Coll Med (Homeo).
Chamberlin, M. P.	23, 6m.	Virginia City '77-'79.	Unk/Med Coll St Louis (Homeo).
Chamblin, Marquis R.	17, 4, 6d, 6l, 6n, 6p, 26, 24.	Austin, LC '66-'67, Eureka '73-'81, Died Decoto, Calif '21.	Ky/Jefferson Med Coll, Cooper Med Coll.
Chapin, Samuel © Farnum	4, 21, 23, 29 (9.22.75), 63.	SC '75, US Army '65, Died Auburn, Calif 3.14.89.	NY (Mich?)/ U Mich, Med Inst Yale.
Chase, Albert	21, 6d, 6p, 6o, 4.	Austin, LC '66-'72, Died Downieville, Calif '02.	NY/(Allopath).
Chase, Reuben H.	4, 6k, 6l.	Reno '77-'78.	Unk/Detroit Homeo Med Coll.
Chowder, H. C.	68.	Pioche, LC '91.	Unk.

Clark, Elizabeth	3, 82, 83 (Fall '73).	Ward, WPC '80.	Unk/(Homeo).
Clark, F. M.	57.	WPC '96.	Unk.
Clark, James Thomas	30, 40.	WC & Carson City '90.	Unk/Rush Med Coll.
Clawson, William	2, 21.	Wellington Station, EC '70.	Unk.
Cleburne, Joseph	9, 21, 2, 6e.	Virginia City '68.	Ireland/Unk.
Collean, D.	39.	Hamilton, WPC '77.	Unk.
Colleau, Louis	2, 21, 6e.	Hamilton, WPC '70.	France/(Phy, Druggist).
Collier, Dr.	6o.	Austin, LaC '71-'72.	Unk.
Collins, D. B.	2, 21, 6f, 6h, 6j, 6k, 6m, 6o, 3, 63.	Virginia City '70-'87.	Ohio (Ky?)/Unk.
Conn, Frank M.	8, 4, 23, 6f, 24, 6i, 6l, 6m, 6n, 3.	Virginia City '62-'87.	Ohio/ Cincinnati Med Coll.
Conn (Cohn), Fetterman W.	4, 8, 6g, 6h, 6j, 6l, 6m, 6n, 3, 63.	Virginia City '73-'81.	Ohio/(Allopath).
Connolly, Pa	1, 21, 6a, 6c, 6h, 6p, 63.	Virginia City '60-'67, Eureka, '72-'75.	Canada/Unk.
Cook, Eliza	21, 10, 19 (picture), 43, 46 (picture), 64, Birth Cert (3.1.87), 64.	Sheridan, DC '99, Prob '84, Died Nev 10.2.47.	Ut/Cooper Med Coll.
Cornell, Dr.	9.	Virginia City '70.	Unk (Drug store).
Counsellor, Charles Eyne	7.	EC '89.	England/Soc Apothecary.
Cox, Thomas H.	31.	Health Off/ Assayer Sutro Tunnel, LyC '76.	Unk/Toland Med Coll.
Crane (Crain), S. E.	12, 21, 2, 6o, 39, 57.	Treasure City, WPC '69, Elko '70-'77.	NY/Unk.
Cummings, William Chielester	24, 30.	Eureka '73, Carson City '77.	Ohio/Geneva Med Coll, NY.

Cummings, John	2, 39, 63.	Hamilton, WPC '70-'77, EuC '75.	Ohio/Unk.
Cummings J.	17, 21.	Austin, LC '65.	NY/Unk.
Curless, William S.	6o.	Wadsworth, WC '71-'72.	Unk.
Daggett, Charles D.	1, 4, 21, 25, 24.	Carson City '55, Eagle Valley, '59, Genoa '60.	Vt/Berkshire Med Coll, Mass, (Also a lawyer).
Dale, H. W.	1, 21.	Carson City '60.	Ohio/Unk.
Darragh, R. C.	6i.	Washoe City '75.	Unk.
Davidson, Dr.	8.	Carson City '75.	Unk.
Davidson, F. (L.?)	3.	Aurora, EC Hosp '77.	La/Unk.
Davidson, Joseph R.	4, 21.	NC '82, Died SF, Calif 1925.	Unk/Toland Med Coll.
Davieson, Daniel (David)	23, 6m.	Virginia City '78-'79.	Unk/Eclectic Med Coll NYC.
Davis, Lafayette L.	20, 4.	ElC '75.	Unk/(Allopath).
Davis, M. A.	64 (Temp lic).	Wadsworth, WC '00.	Unk/Jefferson Med Coll.
Davis, M. J.	57.	WPC "92'- '98.	Unk.
Davis, Magnet J.	21, 18, 26, 64, 68.	Golconda, HC '99, Eureka '00, Pioche, LC '05.	Unk/Cincinnati Coll Med Surg.
Davison, Henry B.	7, 30, 6k, 6l, 6n.	Carson City '75-'78, Aurora, EC '78-'81.	Unk/Jefferson Med Coll.
Dawson, Alson	8, 21, 6f, 24, 6l, 6m, 40. (Half bro H. H. Hogan).	Reno '73-'87, 1st Supt St Hosp '82, Supt Schools	NY/Cooper Med Coll.
Day, J. H.	6a.	Virginia City '62.	Unk.

Deal, David L.	20, 4, 8, 21, 6l, 6o, 18, 2, 39, 25, 63, 68.	Treasure City '70-'72, Pioche, LC '72-'77, Tuscarora, ElC '78, Eureka Co, LyC '75.	Md/Cooper Med Coll.
De Forrest, Mrs. Brown	6n.	Virginia City '80- '81.	Unk.
De Freye, B. Charles	4, 30, 26, 40, 3.	WC, Carson City & Eureka '79-'80.	Belguim/Eclectc Med Coll NYC, Med Soc Calif Med Surg, SF.
Dehl, Dr.	17.	Austin, LC '65.	Unk.
De La Mar, H. M.	21, 25.	Nev '97.	NH/Unk.
De La Matye, Elias B.	4, 6n, 26, 3.	Eureka '79-'80, Died Sacra- mento, Calif '29.	NY/Cleveland Homeo Occiden- tal Med Coll.
Delavan, "Doc" James	9, 6i.	Virginia City '75- '91.	Unk.
DeLong, C. E.	21, 63.	HC '75.	La/Unk.
Denny, Franklin M.	21, 6h, 26, 63.	EuC '72-'75.	Ohio/Rush Med Coll.
De Wolfe, Charles Lord	20, 11.	ElC '75.	Unk/Amer U (Eclectic) Phila- delphia.
Dobrenz, Adolph Edwin	2, 21, 6g, 6h, 6o, 26, 63.	Virginia City '70- '72, Eureka '75.	Germany/U Würtburg.
Donner, F.	1, 21, 6p.	Virginia City '60- '67.	Va (R.I?)/Unk.
Donovan, F.	2, 21, 6g.	Gold Hill, SC '70, Virginia City '71.	Conn/Unk.
Dougan, W. McKay	21, 25, 38.	Nev '97.	Unk/U Louisville Med Dept.
Downer (Donner), Fenno	1, 6a, 6c, 21.	Virginia City '60- '62.	Conn/Unk.
Drake, Frank A.	20 (picture), 11, 21, 6l, 6n, 26, 43.	Eureka & Cor- nucopia, ElC '77-'78, Tus- carora, ElC '80- '00.	Tenn/Jefferson Med Coll.

Drew, J. W.	6o.	Mtn City, ElC '71-'72.	Unk.
Dukes, Harrison Colum- bus	18, 4 .	Pioche, LC '90, Died '17.	Unk/Drake U, Des Moines, Iowa.
Dungledaddy, Dr.	17.	Austin, LC, date unk.	Unk.
Dunlevy, J.	21, 63.	LC '75.	Va/Unk.
Dunscombe, E.	63.	WPC '75.	Va/Unk.
Dunyan, J. F.	2.	ElC '70.	Maine/Unk.
Eaton, James M.	40.	WC '89.	Unk/Phy Surg Coll Miss.
Ehrenberg, Dr.	6c.	Virginia City '64.	Unk.
Eickelroff, William H. (Eichelrath)	1, 21, 24.	Aurora, EC, Virginia City & Carson City '60.	Germany/Unk.
Eichler, Dr.	6c.	Virginia City '64.	Unk.
Ellis, Joseph J. (I?).	1, 21, 6b, 6g, 6h, 6p, 24, 29 (3.10.60 & 1.10.63).	Steam Boat Valley, Utah Terr '60-'67, Virginia City '71- '72.	NY/Unk.
Ellis, R. B.	2, 9, 21, 6e, 6h, 6o, 6p.	Reno '68-'72, Carson City '72, Dayton, LyC	Va/Unk.
Ellis, Robert Andrew	23, 4, 40.	Virginia City '84, WC '87, Died Cape Nome, Alaska.	Ohio/Ky Sch Med Louisville, Med Acad Ky.
Ellis, R. P.	6a.	Genoa, DC '63.	Unk.
Emerson, Marcus (Mark)	4, 6a.	Gold Hill, SC '61-'62.	Unk/Cleveland Med Coll, Med Dept West Res Coll.
Engels (Engel), Frederick H.	8, 23, 24, 6k, 6l, 6m, 6n, 3.	Virginia City '72- '81.	Germany/U Jena.

Evans, John M.	23, 4.	Virginia City '76, Died Phoenix, Ariz.	Unk/Starling Med Coll Columbus , Ohio.
Evans, James	10, 21, 64.	Gardnerville, DC '99.	Unk/Balto Med Coll.
Fairfax, Charles S.	6b.	Virginia City '63.	Unk.
Falconer, Alexander Frank	23, 21, 6k, 6l, 63.	Gold Hill, SC '75-'78.	Canada/ Harvard Med Coll.
Fales, M.	6c.	Virginia City '64.	Unk.
Farrow, Edward Dunbar	7, 4, 30.	Carson City & EC '92.	Unk/U Pa.
Fee, Edward	40, 4.	WC '89.	Unk/Detroit Med Coll (Wayne St U).
Fee, George	4, 21, 25, 30, 40, 41, 43, 59, 64, 65. (1st ENT specialist see Hershiser)	Carson City '93, Reno '95-'00.	Canada/Detroit Med Coll (Wayne St U).
Fee, Katherine (Female, maiden name, Van Harlingen)	4, 21, 59, 64.	WC '89-'00.	Ohio/Cooper Med Coll.
Ferguson, H.	2, 21.	Elko '70.	Ky/Unk.
Ferry, Louis	11.	Elko '78.	Unk/Med Coll Cincinnati.
Fetterman, N. P.	68.	Pioche, LC '73.	Unk.
Fetterman, Wilford Washington	7, 4, 23, 6k. 63, 68.	EC '80s, Pioche, LC '73, Virginia City '75-'77.	Pa/Hahnemann Med Coll (Homeo).
Fife, John	30.	Carson City '82.	Unk/U City NY.
Finley, J. L.	6a.	Dayton, LyC '61-'62.	Unk.
Fisher, C. W.	21, 63.	SC '75.	Canada/Unk.
Flattery, Jonathan	23, 40.	Virginia City '75, WC '77.	Unk/Eclectic Med Coll Cincinnati.

Fleming, John E.	20, 11.	Elko '90.	Unk/Kansas City Hosp Coll Med.
Foltz, Charles G.	6o, 39, 68.	Pioche, LC '71-'73, Died in SF, Calif '73.	Unk.
Foltz, William	8, 21, 25.	Pioche, LC '72.	Unk.
Forden, Willim B.	40, 4.	WC '96.	Unk/Eclectic Med Coll Cincinnati.
Forrest, John Murray	23, 4, 21, 6i.	Virginia City '75.	Ireland/ Bellevue Hosp Med Coll.
Forrester, Thomas William	18, 21, 4, 43, 64.	Pioche, LC '90-'00.	Scotland/Wayne St U, Detroit, Detroit Coll Med Surg.
Fowler, Charles	2, 6g.	Gold Hill, SC '70-'71.	NY/Unk.
Fowler, Henry R.	12, 4, 23, 6g, 6i, 6k, 6o, 2, 39, 63.	Elko '70-'71, Virginia City '71-'77.	Mass (Canada)/ Rush Med Coll, Chicago.
Fowler, W. B.	4, 21.	Virginia City '70, SC '75.	Canada (Maine?)/ (Allopath).
Fox, John W.	2, 11, 4, 21, 24, 6l, 6m, 6n, 6h, 39, 43, 63.	Elko '70-'77, Carson City '76-'00.	Pa/Scientific Homeo Coll Med U Pa.
Francis, Loftus Harley	10, 21, 26, 43, 64.	Gardnerville, DC '99, Eureka '07.	England/Calif Med Coll SF, (Eclectic).
Franklin, Luther Theodore	10, 43, 51 (11.20.1936), 52 (5.21.93) , 53.	DC '93-'96.	Sweden/Nat Coll Electro-Therapeutics, Indpls, (Eclectic) Independent Med Coll, Chicago.
Frederick, C. T (H, W?).	21, 6l, 63.	WC '75-'78.	Germany/Unk.
Freeman, Dr.	57.	WPC, Ely '89.	Unk.
Freeman, Gideon M.	40, 4.	WC '94, Calif lic revoked in '15.	Unk/Coll Phy Surg Balto.
Friedriecks, C.(D.) W.	6g, 6h, 6j, 6i, 6o, 2, 19 (11.23.70).	Reno '70-'75.	Germany/Unk.

Fuller, Benjamin F.	20.	Elko '97.	Unk/Amer Eclectic Med Coll Ohio.
Fury, Bryan	1.	Virginia City '60.	Ireland/Unk.
Gager, Edward Finley	39.	Virginia City '77.	Unk/Ky Sch Med.
Galveston, Peter S.	1.	Carson City '60.	Ohio/Unk.
Gardner, George Montgomery	20, 11, 21, 43.	Gold Creek, ElC '96, Elko '97, Reno '21, Fallon '05, SF, Calif '22-'46, Died Berkeley, Calif '70.	Nev '74/Cooper Med Coll.
Gaston, William M.	9, 21, 6e, 6a, 6b, 6c, 32, 6p.	Virginia City, Gold Hill, SC '61-'69.	Unk.
Gates, D. V.	2, 21, 6e, 6g, 6j, 9, 6o.	Virginia City '68-'74.	NY/Unk.
Gautier, L. P.	9, 6b.	Virginia City '63.	Unk.
Geiger, D. M.	21, 6b.	Toll Road '61, Virginia City '63.	Unk.
Geiss, Anna	40.	WC '89.	Unk/Cohner Med Coll, Alsace, Germany.
Geller, William	24.	Belmont, NC '65.	Unk.
George, R. W. T.	2, 21, 6e, 6j, 6o.	Virginia City '70-'74.	England/Unk.
Gerdes, M. J.	64.	Nev '00.	Unk/Calif Med Coll, SF, Calif (Eclectic).
Geyer, D. M.	63.	SC '75.	NY/Unk.
Gibson, A.	59, (Bro of Samuel).	Reno '96.	Unk.
Gibson, Alexander	57.	WPC '99 for 5 wks.	Unk.
Gibson, Samuel Carrol	4, 21, 25, 8, 37, 40, 41, 42, 43, 59, 65, (Bro of A. Gibson).	Supt St Hosp, Reno '95-'00.	Mo/Mo Med School, St Louis.

Gillingham, C. F.	8, 6k, 6m, 6n, 3.	Virginia City '77-'81.	England/Unk.
Giroux, Edward David	43, 64, (Temp lic).	Golconda & Winnemucca, HC '00.	Calif/U Calif.
Glick, J. S.	6m.	Carson City '78-'79.	Unk.
Goetches, J. W.	2, 6h, 39.	Eureka '70-'77.	NY/Unk.
Goodenough, R. A.	3.	Belleville, EC '80.	NY/Unk.
Goodrich, W. E.	1.	Carson City '60.	Vt/Unk.
Gordon, Charles H.	9, 55, 56, 29 (7.15.68), 57 (2.6.69 & 1.23.69).	Virginia City '67-'69, Treasure City, WPC '69.	Unk.
Goss, William H.	6b, 6e, 6c.	Virginia City '63-'68.	Unk.
Graham, J. S.	2, 21.	LyC and NC '70.	NY/Unk.
Grant, Horace S.	23, 4.	Virginia City '90.	Unk/U Pa.
Grant, John	4, 23, 6k, 6m, 3, 65, 24 (picture), 25, 8, 6n.	Virginia City '76-'81.	Canada/Albany Med Coll, Jefferson Med Coll, Royal Coll Surg London.
Green, C. C.	9, 6e, 6c, 6g, 6h, 6j, 32, 6p, 6o, 2, 39, 86.	Virginia City '64-'77.	Ohio/Unk.
Gregory, Jacob R.	21, 4.	Reno, date unk.	NY/Coll Phy Surg NY
Grey, Georgia (Mrs. W. S.)	6f, 3, 57.	Hamilton, WPC '80-'87.	Unk.
Grindley, Thomas R.	30, 6k, 6l, 4.	Carson City '75-'78.	Unk/Jefferson Med Coll.
Grover, A. J.	21, 6i, 40, 63.	WC '75.	Pa/Eclectic Med Inst & Rock Is Med School.
Groves, I. N	6o.	Unionville, HC '71-'72.	Unk.
Groves, Pat	2.	HC '70.	Ohio/Unk.

Grub, T. L.	24.	LaC '62.	Unk.
Guffin, James A.	9, 6f, 6e, 6d, 6k, 6l, 6n, 6m.	Austin, LaC '66, Virginia City '77-'87, Co Phy '67.	Unk.
Guinan, James W.	9, 21, 4, 8, 25, 30, 6f, 64, 67.	Virginia City, Carson City '82-'99.	Unk/U Mich.
Gunn, John William	27.	Battle Mtn, LaC '86.	Unk/Cooper Med Coll.
Hagar, (James) Henry	4, 6l, 6n, 6f, 18, 26, 43, 64, 57.	Hamilton, WPC '78-'81, Supt Schools '78, Eureka '85-'87, Pioche, LC '96-'99, Cherry Ck, WPC '00, Died Ruby Valley, ElC '29	Unk/Iowa Med Coll, Keokuk, Iowa.
Hall, Albert Cook	20, 4, 11, 6l, 6n.	Elko '75, Carlin, ElC '76-'81.	Canada/ Dartmouth Med.
Hall, James U. (W?)	9, 8, 6e, 6b, 6i, 6k, 6l, 6m, 6n, 6o, 39, 3, 63.	Virginia City '63, Gold Hill, SC '68-'81.	Ky/Unk.
Hamilton, A.	2.	LaC '70.	Ill/Unk.
Hamilton, G (S).	21, 63.	EuC '75.	Ohio/Unk.
Hamilton, James A.	40.	WC '97.	Unk/Indep Med Coll Ill.
Hammon, S. C.	21, 1, 6a.	Virginia City '60.	Mass/Unk.
Hammond, Charles Lewis	21, 4, 24, 18, 26, 64, 57.	Tonopah '95, WPC '98, Pioche, LC '97, Eureka '98-'99, Sumpter, Oreg '00, Died Tonopah '10.	Ill/Coll Phy Surg Chicago.
Hammond, Josiah Shaw	21, 4, 24, 6l, 6n, 9, 18, 27, 68.	Nev pre '65, Pioche, LC '75, NC '78, Austin, LaC '79-'85, Died Mont '28.	Mass/Cooper Med Coll.
Hanenberg (Harenberg, Hornberg), C.	21, 18, 68.	Pioche, LC pre '65, Pioche '73, LC '75.	Germany/Unk.

Han, Abbert	3.	Elko '80.	Canada/Unk.
Hanson, Thomas C.	22, 21, 4, 6f, 6n, 15, 3, 63.	Winnemucca, HC '75-'81, Died Winnemucca '02.	Maine/Toland Med Coll.
Harcourt, Luke A.	64.	Carson City '00.	Unk/Med Dept. U Buffalo.
Harmony, Peter	40, 4.	WC '88.	Unk/Eclectic Med Coll Calif.
Harris, Elias Braman	1, 23, 6k, 6l, 63, 9, 24 (picture), 25, 6m, 6n, 67.	Virginia City '59, Gold Hill, SC '60, Civil War, Virginia City '75-'81, Died '00.	NY/NY Med Coll, Whitokes School Surg.
Harrison, G. W.	21, 6h.	Verdi, WC '70, Reno '72.	Va/Unk.
Harrison, J. Charles	23, 4.	Virginia City '87.	Unk/Bennett Coll Eclectic Med Surg Chicago.
Hartzell, I. N.	6a.	Virginia City '62.	Unk.
Hascall, Charles A.	7, 4.	EC '96, Died Fallon '28.	Unk/College Science (Eclectic) LA, Calif.
Hastings, Carrie B. Flower	23, 4.	Virginia City '92, Died Sedalia, Mo.	Unk/Kansas City Hosp Coll Med.
Hatch, Dr.	24.	Austin '63.	Unk.
Hausen, Thomas H.	64.	Winnemucca, HC '99	Unk/Toland Med Coll.
Hay, Henry	21, 6e.	Virginia City '68-'69.	Unk.
Hayden, Thomas M.	6l, 38, 40.	Wadsworth, WC '77-'78.	Unk/Coll Phy Surg, Keokuk, Iowa.
Hazlett, John Clark	21, 25, 6e, 6b, 6g, 3, 31, 6p, 9, 6o, 2, 39, 24, 63, 65, 84.	Dayton, LyC '62-'72-'80, Supt & Phy Sutro Tunnel '85, Nev Senator '71-'75, Died Dayton, Nev '95.	Pa/Winchester Med Coll, Winchester, Va.

Heanna, W. J.	20.	Wells, ElC '94.	Unk.
Heath, Mark W.	9, 6c, 6e, 6h, 6j, 6k, 6m, 6n, 6o, 2, 39.	Gold Hill, SC '66-'69,Virginia City '71-'81.	NY/Unk.
Hempel, Gustav	4, 6g, 6h.	Carson City '71-'72.	Unk /(Allopath).
Henderson, Joseph Jefferson	20, 11.	ElC '93, Member of 1st St Bd Health.	Unk/U Mich.
Hennessy, J. C.,	67.	Carson City '98	Unk.
Hennessy, Thomas James	21, 4, 27, 43, 64.	Battle Mtn, LaC '98, Reno '99, Austin, LaC '00, Died Reno '15.	Ireland/Royal Coll Surg, Ireland.
Herdan, Moscu I,	27, 40.	WC '91, Battle Mtn, LaC '92.	Unk/U Bucharest.
Hep, C. G. (A.)	1, 21.	Silver City, LyC '60.	Germany/Unk.
Hereford, R. (F.) H.	6e, 6c.	Gold Hill, SC '64, Austin, LaC '67.	Unk.
Herndon, E. L.	6c.	Virginia City '64.	Unk..
Herrick, Hamis S.	21, 24, 6h, 6l, 6h, 39, 3, 66 ('57), 57.	Nev '60, Hamilton, WPC '69-'91, Supt Schools, WPC phy, Died Hamilton, Nev 2.21.91.	NY/Cooper Med Coll.
Herrick, Loyal A.	21, 24, 6j, 30, 6i, 6l, 3, 6m, 52 (11.2.88 and 5.2.90).	Carson City '72-'90.	NY/(Homeo).
Herrick, R. C.	47.	Austin '64.	Unk.
Hershiser, Anthony Emmet	21, 4, 25, 40, 41, 43, 64, 65.	Reno '98-'00, 1st ENT see Geo Fee, Died Reno '21.	Ohio/Jefferson Med Coll, Miami Med Coll, Cincinnati.
Hey, Henry	2.	WPC '70.	France/Unk.
Hickox, W. H.	3.	Reno '80.	NY/Unk.

Hiller, Frederick Jr.	9, 4, 6c, 6e, 6p, 6o.	Virginia City '64- '72,Died LA, Calif '24.	Unk/ Hahnemann Med Coll (Homeo).
Hiller, D. A.	57.	Virginia City & Treasure City, WPC '69.	Unk/(Homeo).
Hinkle, J. M.	30.	Carson City '78.	Unk/Luguse U, NY.
Hodgins, Frederick W.	38.	Virginia City '99.	Unk/Victoria Med Coll, Ontario.
Hoffman, Doctress	29 (4.12.65), 86.	Virginia City '65.	Unk/Educated in Germany.
Hogan, Henry Hardy	8, 21, 4, 25, 6e, 6h, 6j, 6i, 6k, 6l, 6m, 6n, 6o, 40, 42, 39, 43, 63, 65, 58 (picture), 66 ('95), 84.	Reno '70-'00, WC Phy '74, Washoe City '64, WPC '75, Nev Assemb '71, '75 &'95, Died Reno '02.	Vt (Ky?)/U Vt Med Coll (Burlington Acad).
Hoit, Doc	9.	Virginia City '69.	Unk.
Holdsworth, J. W.	6j.	Virginia City '73- '74.	Unk.
Holmes, M.	6c, 6n.	Virginia City '64- '81.	Unk.
Holmes, Thomas B.	40.	WC '95.	Unk/Med Soc Colo (Eclectic).
Holtz, J. P. L.	27.	Battle Mtn, LaC '82.	Unk/Calif Med Coll (Eclectic), Oakland.
Hood, Charles John	21, 20, 4, 11, 27, 37, 64. (Bro of Wm Henry)	Battle Mtn, LaC '87, Elko '94, Died LA, Calif '31.	Mich/U Mich, Iowa Med Coll Keokuk, Iowa.
Hood, William Henry	21, 27, 41, 42, 64. (Bro of Chas John)	Battle Mtn, LaC '86-'99, VP BME '99.	Mich/U Mich.
Hopkins, Henry St. George Lyons	20, 21, 4, 23, 6g, 6j, 6k, 6o, 39, 63.	Elko '69, Virginia City '71-'77.	Ky (Va?)/U Pa.
Howe, Edward	2.	WPC '70.	Ky/Unk.

Hudson, W. V.	6a.	Carson City '61-'62.	Unk/(Homeo).
Hudson, M. V.	24.	Elko '69.	Unk.
Huffaker, Anthony	9, 21, 25, 30, 41, 64, 65, 67.	Carson City '96-'99, (Pediatrics).	Unk/Cooper Med Coll.
Hunter, George F.	40, 4.	WC '95.	Unk/U Buffalo.
Hunter, James Albert	4, 30, 40.	WC & Carson City '79, Died Tex '22.	Canada/Med Bd Upper Canada, Eclectic Med Soc Calif.
Huntington, Thomas Waterman	20, 11, 4, 25, 61, 6n, 3, 61.	Elko '76-'78, Pres CMA, Tuscarora, ElC '78-'81, Sacramento, Calif '81, Wells '97, UCSF '99, Died SF, Calif '29.	Ill/Harvard Med Coll.
Huntsman, Charles R.	27, 4.	Battle Mtn, LaC '77.	Unk/Iowa So West Med Assoc (Eclectic).
Huntsman, J. A.	21, 4, 6h, 61, 6n, 63.	Battle Mtn, LaC '72-'75, Austin, LaC '78-'81, Died Austin '04.	Pa/Iowa Med Coll, Keokuk, Iowa.
Hurd, P. W.	21, 63.	Elko '75.	NY/Unk.
Hutchins, Frederick	4, 61, 6m, 40, 63, 22.	HC '75, Reno '78-'79.	Maine/ Dartmouth Med Coll.
Hutton, , Robert C.	20.	Owyhee, Duck Valley Res, ElC '81.	Unk.
Hylton, T. A.	24.	Mormon Station (Genoa) '51.	Unk.
Ingerson, Augustus W.	12, 4, 60, 2, 39.	Elko '70-'77.	Ky/Eclectic Med Coll, Cincinnati.
Inman, Edward Lorimer	30.	Carson City '98.	Unk/Med Coll Miami, Cincinnati.
Jackman, Enoch A.	21, 4, 40, 41, 43.	WC '86, Wadsworth, WC '99-'00, Died Wadsworth '21.	NH/U Vt.

James, Bruce	21.	Carson City '70.	Maine/Unk.
James, W. B.	68.	Pioche, LC '72-'73.	Unk.
Jennings, Charles W.	21, 63.	NC '75 Delamar, LC '06.	England/Unk.
Jennison, John Egbert	21, 18, 43, 64.	Pioche, LC & Delamar, LC '99-'02.	Minn/U Minn Coll Med Surg.
Jessup, Dr.	20.	Wells, ElC '80.	Unk.
Johnson, D. H.	22, 61.	Winnemucca '75-'78.	Unk.
Johnson, Barton Willard	21, 27, 64.	Battle Mtn, LaC '95, Carson City '99.	Unk/Barnes Med Coll, Saint Louis.
Johnson, J. Thomas	9, 21, 23, 24, , 61, 6m, 40.	Reno '76 & Virginia City '78-'79.	Unk/U Md.
Jones, Dr.	22.	Unionville, HC '75.	Unk.
Jones, Helena (Doctress and Accoucheur)	21, 6o, 39, 57.	Treasure City, WPC '69-'77.	Denmark/Unk.
Jones, Lemuel Frank	64 (Temp lic).	Nev '00.	Unk/U Pa.
Jones, W. B.	2, 6p, 22.	Dayton, LyC '67, Unionville, HC '70-'75.	Pa/Unk.
Joseph, Lionel B.	26.	Eureka '79.	Unk/Columbia Coll Phy Surg.
Joy, Oliver	3.	Carson City '80.	Canada/Unk.
Kearney, G. Joseph	30.	Carson City '79.	Unk/McGill U Coll Med.
Kearney, William H.	6n, 3.	Carson City '80.	Canada/Unk.
Keeler, H.	6c.	Virginia City '64.	Unk.
Keene, Edward R.	21, 18, 26, 64.	Pioche, LC & Eureka '99.	Unk/Curtis Physio-Med Coll (Eclectic), Indpls (Phy, Pharm).

Kent, L. A.	6f.	Winnemucca, HC '87.	Unk.
Keyser, P. W.	6p.	Virginia City '67.	Unk.
Killpatrick, Joseph	2, 3, 6o, 49 (10.27.80), 50 (12.2.65, 54 (12.6.78).	Genoa, DC '65- '78, Insane in '78.	NY/(Minister and Doctor Physic).
Kincaid, Dr.	20.	Carlin, ElC '70.	Unk.
King, Benjamin L.	25, 24, 8.	Utah Terr '52, Eagle Valley, (King's Canyon) '59.	NY/Unk.
King, Frank D.	43.	Washoe '00.	Calif/Unk.
King, H. Volney	38.	Tonopah, NC '99.	Unk.
King, Samuel A.	30.	Carson City '81.	Unk/Homeo Med Coll, Cleveland.
Kinkead, Alex	6h.	Elko '72.	Unk.
Kirby, Paul T.	9, 21, 23, 6f, 6g, 6l, 6m, 6o, 3, 63, 29 (9.22.75).	Virginia City SC Hosp '70, Silver City, LyC '71- '72, Gold Hill, SC '75-'80, Died '88.	NY/Eclectic Med Soc Ill.
Kirch, E. J.	6m.	Virginia City '78- '79.	Unk.
Kistler, Washington Lincoln	21, 4, 40, 43.	Wadsworth, WC '96-'00, Died Sparks '21.	Pa/U Buffalo.
Knapp, Henry K.	9, 4, 23, 6g, 6h, 6j, 6k, 6l, 6m, 6n, 6o, 2, 39, 3.	Virginia City '68- '81.	Conn/Cleveland Homeo Med Coll.
Koenig, Theodore T.	7, 4.	EC '94.	Unk/Academy Med, Louisville.
Kords, L.	8.	Galena, LC '62.	Unk.
Kosber, A. Emil	23.	Virginia City '76.	Unk/U Calif.
Kun, Edwin E.	43.	Eureka '00.	Wisc/Unk.

Name	References	Location	Origin/Education
Lackey Howard	43.	Gold Hill, SC '00.	Nev/Unk.
Laird, S. A. (Morton)	2, 60, 39.	Austin, LC '70-'77.	NY/Unk.
Lathrop George D.	23, 4, 30, 40.	WC, Carson City & Virginia City '92, Wash '84.	Unk/NW Coll Med, Chicago.
Lathrop, H. P.	23, 24.	Elko '69, Coroner.	Unk.
Leary, Joseph Weight	23, 61.	Virginia City '77-'78.	Unk/Queens U, Ireland.
Leavitt, Granville Irving	3, 7, 21, 4, 8, 6n, 36, 37, 42, 43, 84.	Pizen Switch (Yerington) '77-, Mason Valley, LyC '75-'00, Nev Senate '97-'01.	Maine/Toland Med Coll.
Lee, Benjamin Brooks	23, 4.	Virginia City '85, Calif lic revoked, Prison, Died SF, Calif '17.	Unk/S.C. Med Coll, Charleston.
Lee, Simeon Lemuel	2, 3, 9, 25, 6f, 61, 64, 24 (picture), 6h, 30, 6n, 18, 26, 37 (picture), 43, 63, 65, 67, 68.	Pioche, LC, '72-'79, Eureka '79, Carson City '79-'27, Sec BME '99, Pres 1 st St Bd Health '93, Died Carson City '27.	Ill/Eclectic Med Coll, Cincinnati (Physio-Med Inst).
Lee, William G.	9.	Virginia City '64.	Unk.
Lefevre, J. B. B.	21, 23, 6e, 6j, 6i, 6k, 61, 60, 39.	Virginia City '65-'78.	France/ (Druggist, phy, accoucher).
Le Guen, Thomas	21, 23, 6g, 6h, 6j, 6i, 2, 6k, 61, 60, 39.	Virginia City '70-'78.	La/Columbia Med Coll NYC.
Legnent, M.	63.	SC '75.	Germany/Unk.
Lewis, John Alexander	42, 21, 4, 25, 64, 65, 37 (picture), 40, 3, 43.	Supt St Hosp '78, Reno '00, Pres NSMA '09, Member 1st St Bd Health '93.	Plumas Co, Calif/ Long Is Coll Hosp.
Loon, Lington	39.	Virginia City '77.	Unk.
Livingston, Henry D.	23, 61.	Virginia City '78.	Unk/U Mich.

Losey, Mahlon F.	40, 4.	WC '93.	Unk/ Eclectic Med Coll, Cincinnati.
Longshore-Potts, Anna Mary	23, 4.	Virginia City '97, Died San Diego, Calif '12.	Unk/Women's Med Coll Pa.
Louder, Austin J.	18, 68.	Pioche, LC '89-'91, Died '91.	Unk/Jefferson Med Coll.
Lucas, George L.	11, 6n.	Elko '77-'81.	Unk/Jefferson Med Coll.
Luce, Charles Baker	21, 20, 4, 11, 10, 6o, 6g, 6m, 2, 39, 64, 52 (11.18.92), 49 (10.27.80), (picture) Carson Valley Hist Soc.	Washoe City, WC '70, Elko '73, Genoa, DC '99, Carson City '71-'00, Died Genoa 10.10.00.	Maine/Bowdoin Med Coll, Maine.
Lukens, Joseph Hamilton	4, 6h, 6n, 6o, 26, 39.	Eureka '71-'81, Died Seattle, Wash '10.	Unk/Eclectic Med Coll NY
Luthes, Daniel	2, 6o, 21, 39.	Unionville, HC '70-'77.	Pa/Unk.
Mackay, Robert M.	1, 21.	Silver City, LyC '60.	Va/Unk.
Mackay, R. W.	1.	Silver City, LyC '60.	Va/Unk.
MacIntosh, Hugh	23.	Virginia City '75.	Unk/Royal Coll Surg, Ireland.
Magee, Thomas James	4, 24, 23, 6k, 6l, 6m.	Gold Hill, SC '77-'79.	Unk/Jefferson Med Coll.
Mangan, Patrick Joseph	27, 21, 43.	Battle Mtn, LaC '98-'00.	Scotland/Cooper Med Coll.
Manley, James F.	2, 4, 20, 21.	Elko '70, Mineral City '71-'72, EC '75.	NC/Cooper Med Coll.
Manning, C.	63.	SC '75	NH/Unk.
Manning, Dr.	2, 21.	Pine Grove, EC '70.	Ind/Unk.
Manotto, Jim	2.	ElC '70.	Canada/Unk.
Manson, John	21, 4, 8, 23, 64, 6k, 6l, 6m, 6n.	Virginia City '75-'81, Gold Hill, SC '75.	Canada/Victoria Coll, Ontario.

Manson, L. Peter	9, 21, 23, 25, 61, 6f, 6j, 6i, 6k, 6m, 6n, 6o, 39, 43, 63, 67, 85.	Virginia City '70-'77, Gold Hill, SC '73, Fresno, Calif '89, Died Fresno '15.	Canada/Victoria Coll, U Mich.
Mantor, Dr.	68.	Pioche, LC '92	Unk.
Marison, Dr.	21 (Not in '70 census).	Virginia City '70s.	Unk.
Marotte (Marotte), Anton	7, 4, 21, 61, 6n, 63.	Columbus, EC '76-'81.	Canada/Victoria Coll, Ontario, Canada.
Marrotte, L.	68.	Pioche, LC '87.	Unk.
Marshall, Dr.	21 (Not in '70 census).	Virginia City '70.	England/Unk.
Martin, Charles H.	12, 20, 57.	Wells, ElC '87, Cherry Creek, WPC '89-'91, SF '91.	Unk.
Mason, Dr.	9.	Gold Hill, SC '76.	Unk.
Mason, B. S.	24, 6p, 39.	EC '64-'67, Pine Grove, LyC '77.	Unk.
Mason, Joseph Ritner	23, 4, 3.	Virginia City '80.	Pa/Jefferson Med Coll.
Mathews George C.	23, 6m, 6n, 18, 68.	Calif '76, Virginia City '78-'79, Gold Hill, SC '80-'81, Pioche, LC '81-'83.	Unk/Royal Coll Surg, Ireland.
Mayo, Harry Nathanial	18, 68.	Pioche, LC '96-'97.	Unk/Baltimore Med Coll.
McCarty, A. G.	21, 63.	Elko '75.	Ind/Unk.
McClary, Del	30, 40.	WC & Carson City '91.	Unk/U City NY.
McCune, David C.	21, 40, 63.	LC '75, WC '76.	Pa/Coll Pa.
McDonald, J.	21, 63.	LC '75.	England/Unk.
McDonald, Terry	63.	SC '75.	Ga/Unk.

McDonald, Thomas Patrick	23, 4, 43, 67.	Virginia City '92-'00, Died SF, Calif.	Maine/U Pa.
McDowell, Samuel S.	21, 20 (picture), 11.	Nev '89, Died Mo '14.	Unk/Med Dept U Cincinnati.
McGarver, Mary	43.	Golconda, HC '00.	Pa/Unk.
McIntire, Byron	40.	WC '94.	Unk/Long Is Coll Hosp.
McKee, Albert Brown	20, 11.	Tuscarora, ElC '87.	Unk/Cooper Med Coll.
McKenzie, D. Banks	3.	Reno '80.	Scotland/Unk.
McKinney, A.	2, 21.	Bruno City, ElC '70.	Ohio/Unk.
McLaren, William Melleville	7.	EC '97.	Unk/Eclectic Med Coll, Madison, Wisc .
McLaughlin, J. J.	24.	Eureka (Secret Canon) '69.	Unk (Miner).
McLean, Daniel (Donald)	8, 22, 21, 23, 61, 63.	Virginia City '75-'78, Unionville, PC '75.	Scotland/ Harvard Med Coll.
Mclelland, H. K.	68.	Pioche, LC '87.	Unk.
McLuestin, Charles A.	43.	Washoe '00.	Maine/Unk.
McMeans, Sheldon A.	9, 21, 24, 6e, 6j, 6p, 6o, 39, 57.	Virginia City '60-'77, Silver Springs, LyC '69, Hamilton, WPC '71-'72, WC '70, Died '76.	Tenn/(Former Trea Calif).
McMullen (McMillen), W. T (F).	3, 63.	Elko '75-'80.	Pa/Unk.
McMurtrey, A. T.	6n.	Virginia City '80-'81.	Unk/(Sold Patent Medicine).
McSwegan, Daniel	40, 4.	WC '98, Died San Diego, Calif.	Ireland/Cooper Med Coll.
Mehan, Dr.	6p.	Aurora, EC '67.	Unk.

Meigs, John Jerrold	12, 4, 11, 6f, 6h, 6l, 6n, 6o, 39, 2, 39.	Elko '70-"81, Died SF, Calif '22.	Vt/Harvard Med Coll.
Melton, Lewis	40, 4.	WC '78, Died Wheatland, Calif '04.	Unk/Iowa Med Coll, Keokuk , Iowa
Meyer, I.L. (Genoa with Herrick)	52 (11.2.88).	Genoa, DC '88.	Unk.
Midleton, S.A.	3.	Aurora, EC '77.	Ala/Unk.
Millar, William S.	11, 6l.	Elko '77, Tus- carora, ElC '78.	Unk/U La.
Millard, Emig L.	21, 2.	Shermantown, WPC '70.	Mass/Unk.
Miller, H. J.	6a.	Virginia City '62.	Unk.
Miller, W. M.	40.	WC '95.	Unk/Cooper Med Coll.
Millhoue, W. F.	64 (Temp lic).	Nev '00.	Unk/Calif Med Coll SF (Eclectic).
Minneer, William S.	6a, 6b, 84.	Virginia City '61- '63, Nev Terr Legislature '62.	Unk.
Mintie, Alexander E.	23, 4.	Virginia City '85, Died Buffalo, NY	Unk/U Pa.
Mitchell, A. H.	6b.	Aurora, EC '63.	Unk.
Mitchell, A. P.	21, 25, 6e, 8, 6g, 6o.	Washoe City '68- '72.	NY/Unk.
Mitchell, J. F.	39.	Virginia City '77.	Unk.
Montezuma, Carlos (Native Born Indian)	20, 11, 14.	West Shoshone Res, Owyhee, ElC '92.	Ariz/Chicago Med Coll NW U.
Mooklar, James P.	4, 6h.	Carson City '72.	Unk/Med Coll Ohio, Cincinnati Med Coll.
Moore, Dr. (with Wixom)	6o.	Austin, LaC '71- '72.	Unk.
Moore, Charles W.	1, 24.	Carson City '60.	Mass/Unk.

Moore, James E.	40.	WC '97.	Unk/Eclectic Med Coll Milkaukee.
Moore, Samuel Grant	7, 6l, 6n, 39, 21, 63.	Belmont, EC '77-'83, Tybo, NC '81.	NJ/Jefferson Med Coll.
Moore, William Leander	7, 2, 64.	EC '94-, Pres NSMS '05.	Unk/Cooper Med Coll.
Morse, Silas E.	40.	WC '99.	Unk/U Kansas City, Mo.
Morton, T. M..	17, 6e, 6d, 6p.	Austin, LC '65-'67.	Unk.
Mullen, C. L.. (J.)	9, 40.	WC & Virginia City '89.	Unk/Miss Med Coll.
Mullinuix, L. P.	64.	Garderville, DC '00	Unk/ Cent Coll P & S, Indpls.
Munckton , George	2, 6e, 24, 6l, 6p, 29 (11.26.59), 6g, 39, 84.	Carson City '59-'78, 3rd Assemb '67.	Ohio/Unk.
Murphy, Daniel	6a.	Carson City '61-'62.	Unk.
Murphy, N. S.	17, 6d, 6p.	Austin, LC '65-'67.	NY/Unk.
Murphy, Henry	6j, 6i.	Reno '74-'75.	Unk.
Nelson, W. J.	68.	Pioche, LC '98.	Unk.
Nesbitt, James A.	24, 21, 4, 6h, 6l, 6n, 6o, 26, 2, 3, 63, 68.	Eureka '69-'81, Pioche, LC '88-'91.	Canada/McGill U Coll Med.
Newland, Ruth E.	23, 4.	Virginia City '82.	Unk/Med Eclectic Coll Cincinnati.
Newton, Dr.	9.	Virginia City '73.	Unk.
Nichols, W. H.	43.	Dun Glen, PC '00.	NJ/Unk.
Norris, Urban H.	21, 18, 64.	Pioche, LC & Elko '99, Refused to pay for Nev lic.	Unk/Omaha Med Coll.
Notewase, C. W.	2.	Ormsby Co '70.	NY/Unk.

O'Byrne, John Mortimer	4, 30.	Carson City '97, Died Ocean View, Calif '99.	Unk/Calif Eclectic Med Coll, SF, Calif.
Oliver, J. W.	6f.	Reno '87.	Unk.
Olmsted, Amos Cameron	42, 21, 20, 11, 33, 64. (picture NE Hist Soc)	Wells '97, Regent U of Nev, NSMS Pres '32, Died Wells '43.	Ill/Cooper Med Coll.
O'Neil, T. D.	68.	Pioche, LC '73.	Unk, bought a saloon.
Owen, D.	6f.	Eureka '87.	Unk.
Owen, J . R. N.	6c, 21, 24, 6h, 6n, 6o, 26, 39, 63, 64.	Virginia City '64-, Hamilton, WPC '72-'77, Eureka '81-'99.	Va/Transylvania U, Lexington, Ky.
Packer. F. G	63.	SC '75.	Mass/Unk.
Packer, Frederick Herbert	21, 4, 23, 24, 6k, 6l, 6m, 6n, 9, 3, 43, 29 (9.22.75).	Virginia City '74-'00.	Vt/ Hahnemann Med Coll (Homeo).
Patterson, William Henry	21, 25, 40, 64, 65.	WC '99, Supt St Hosp.	Unk/Bd Med Soc Calif (Eclectic).
Paugh, W. J.	57.	Treasure City, WPC '69.	Unk.
Peabody, W. F.	6c.	Virginia City '64.	Unk.
Peake, H.	6c.	Virginia City '64.	Unk.
Perkins, Edward T.	24, 8.	Pyr Lake War '60.	Unk.
Peterson, Fred J.	40.	WC '96.	Unk/Wisc Ed Med Co.
Pettit, Marshall	26, 27, 4.	Battle Mtn, LaC '95, Eureka '95.	Unk/Med Coll Ind, Butler U, Indpls.
Petty, James W.	20, 11.	Wells, ElC '89.	Unk/U Louisville.
Phelan, Chauncy	21 (Not in '70 census).	Treasure City, WPC '70.	Pa/Unk.

Phillips, Percy Todd	21, 25, 30, 40, 43, 59, 65, 64. (Bro of William)	WC '89, Carson City '92, Reno '95-'00, 1st Pres BME.	Ohio/Cleveland Med Coll, Med Dept West Res Coll.
Phillips, William A.	21, 25, 59, 64, 65. (Bro of Percy)	Reno '96-'99.	Unk/Cleveland Med Coll, Med Dept West Res Coll.
Pickard, John Everitt	21, 4, 23, 25, 65, 37 (picture), 41, 67.	Virginia City '92, Pres NSMS '06.	Canada/Victoria Med Coll (Toronto School Med), Ontario.
Pierce, G. W.	21, 63.	LC '75.	England/Unk.
Pilkington, Dr.	9.	Virginia City '67.	Unk.
Pilson, Chauncey F.	8, 21, 24, 60, 18, 3, 25, 63, 68.	Pioche, LC '70-'99, Died in Maxwell, Calif '99.	Pa/Jefferson Med Coll.
Pinkerton, Thomas H.	9, 29, 6a. 6b, 6c, 24, 6p.	Virginia City '61-'67, Co Hosp '64.	Unk.
Pinniger, Sidney Ernest Davis	27, 21.	Battle Mtn, LaC '97.	Unk/Cooper Med Coll.
Pitser, J. S.	6p.	Virginia City '67.	Unk.
Plant, Benjamin Anthony	4, 43.	McDermit, HC '00, Died Santa Cruz, Calif '11.	Chile/Toland Med Coll.
Post-Van Orden, Catherine Nicholas	23, 6n, 46 (picture).	Virginia City '79-'81.	Unk/Cooper Med Coll.
Powell, Barton Jerome	26.	Eureka '94.	Unk/Jefferson Med Coll.
Powell, J. W.	6n.	Paradise, HC '80-'81.	Unk.
Pratt, George Douglas	21, 64.	Reno '99.	Unk/Calif Med Coll (Eclectic).
Prentiss (Prentice), Chalmer Morrel C.	20, 11, 4, 40.	WC & Virginia City '87, Elko '88, Died Tex.	Ohio/U Ohio, U Dorcester, Cleveland, U Wooster Med Dept.

Price (Preis), Charles Wallace	23, 4.	Virginia City '79, Died Richmond, Maine.	Unk/Bowdoin Med Coll, Maine.
Price, Randolph Frederic	21, 23, 6g, 6h, 6j, 6i, 6o, 39, 63.	Nev pre '65, SC '75-'77.	Germany/U Berlin, U Marburg.
Pring, Elijah James	23, 4, 6i, 63.	Virginia City '75, Died Tucumcani, NM.	Ireland/Royal Coll Surg England, Dublin Trinity Coll, Ireland.
Pritchard, Maurice	21, 4, 23, 40. 6l, 6m, 66 ('93, picture).	Virginia City '75-'79, Milk Inspector '78, Died Reno '13.	Canada/U Mich, Detroit Med Coll.
Pugh, John W.	24, 6a, 84.	Aurora, EC '61-'63, 1st & 2nd Nev Terr Legislature Council '61-'62.	Unk.
Quimby, Watson F.	9, 4.	Virginia City, date unk.	Unk/Jefferson Med Coll.
Quinlin, A. G.	6b.	Virginia City '63.	Unk.
Rae, J. H.	9.	Virginia City '86.	Unk.
Randall, Andrew	9.	Virginia City '56, Killed '56.	Unk.
Razsas (Rozsas), Hugo	23, 24.	Virginia City '80, Steamboat Springs, WC '81, Member Calif BME.	Unk/U Munich.
Redman, Joseph Reasor	21, 4, 8, 30, 40, 42, 43.	WC '86, Carson City '88, Reno '95-'00, Died SF, Calif '24.	Ky/Amer Med Coll (Eclectic) Saint Louis Mo.
Reed, Clarence E.	7, 4.	EC '86, Died SF, Calif '29.	Unk/U Calif.
Reese, E. L.	2, 6o, 39.	Mtn City, ElC '70-'77.	Mo/Unk.
Reece, John Henry	21, 6f, 6l, 26, 63, 68.	Eureka '75-'78 & '87, Pioche, LC '84-'87 & '89.	NY/Eclectic Med Inst, Cincinnati.
Rehm, Carl	68.	Pioche, LC '90	Unk.

Renwick, Robert W.	40.	WC '95.	/Mo Med Coll.
Rep, J. C.	21 (Not in '70 census).	Waipas, LC '70.	Maine/Unk.
Rice, William H.	26.	Eureka '76.	Unk/Chicago Med Coll.
Richardson, Abner Stanton	7, 21, 4, 6l, 6n, 36.	Belleville, (MC) '76-'81, Mason Valley, LyC.	Vt/U Pa.
Richardson, Rodney Hall	21, 8, 57.	Wadsworth, WC '77, Ely, WPC '89-'04, WPCo Phy '03, BME '10-'13, Supt St Hosp '21, Died Dalton, Ga '29.	Md/U Pa.
Richey, D. T.	39.	Nev, date unk.	Unk.
Riddle, J. G.	17, 6p.	Austin, LC '65, Ione, NC '67.	Unk.
Robb, F. M.	21, 63.	DC '75.	Ill/Unk.
Roberts, R. R.	2, 6g.	Virginia City '70- '71.	NY/Unk.
Robinson, Benjamin	8, 24, 11, 23, 6l, 25, 30, 6m, 6n, 40, 63, 65, 29 (9.22.75), 64 (Temp lic).	Virginia City '75- '81, Carson City & Elko '83, 1st Sec NSMS '75, WC '94.	England/U City NY
Rochex, James (Joseph)	40, 43.	WC '97, Hawthorne, MC '00.	France/Med Coll Colo (U Colo).
Rockman, Moses	4, 23, 24, 6l, 6n, 26, 3.	Eureka & Virginia City '76, Ward, WPC '78, Eureka Co '80- '81.	Unk/Cooper Med Coll.
Rogers, H. D.	6b.	Virginia City '63.	Unk.
Rogers, William H.	7, 21, 4, 8, 6l, 25, 63, 68.	Pioche, LC '72, SC '75-'77, EC '77-'78.	Md/U Md, Coll Med Balto.
Ross, W. W.	6b.	Genoa, DC '63.	Unk.
Roth, Edward	26, 4.	Eureka '82, Died Miami, Fla '19.	Unk/Bellevue Hosp Med Coll.

Routen, William H.	40.	WC '96.	Unk/St Louis Med Coll.
Sabrizcia, C. B.	21, 63.	LyC '75.	NJ/Unk.
Sabrio, Edmund	30.	Carson City '85.	Unk/U Episcople Coll.
Sailor, Alexis W.	7, 4, 6n, 3.	Belleville and NC '80, EC '92.	Mo/Iowa Med Coll, Keokuk Iowa.
Samuels, William Lee	21, 8, 26, 42, 64 refused to pay for lic.	Eureka '97, Winnemucca, HC '99, Pres NSMS '27, Died Reno '31.	Ind/U Louisville.
Sanborn, F. H.	40.	WC '93.	Unk/U Colo.
Sanborn, Samuel	40.	WC '98.	Unk/Ind Med Coll Ill.
Sanders, H. S.	1.	Virginia City '60.	Ohio/Unk.
Satterlee, Frank Peck	64.	Nev '00.	Unk/Coll P & S, SF (Eclectic).
Sawyer, Dr.	57.	WPC ''90..	Unk.
Schnabel, Martin	9, 23, 4, 61.	Virginia City '77, Gold Hill, SC '78, Died Sacra- mento, Calif '11.	Unk/U Calif.
Scholdesch (Desch), Charles	2, 6g, 6h, 21, 6p, 6o.	Virginia City '67- '72.	France/Unk.
Scott, Dr. (with Goetchus)	6o.	Eureka '71-'72.	Unk.
Scott, C.	2, 21.	Austin, LC '70.	Va/Unk.
Scott, M. B.	21, 4, 6l, 6n, 63.	Austin, LC '75- '81.	Iowa/Unk.
Scott, R. B.	6o.	Ruby Valley, ElC '71-'72.	Unk.
Scott, William Henry Sumner	20.	Elko '99.	Unk/Royal Coll Phy Surg King- ston, Canada.

Seals, Ramlis	3.	Ward, WPC '80.	Ill/Unk.
Seaton, Joseph H.	4, 30, 6m.	Carson City '78-'79.	Unk/Bennett Med Coll Chicago: Eclectic Coll Med Surg, Louisville Inst.
Seltzer, C.	21 (Not in '70 census).	Nev '70, Died WC overdose Morphine.	NY/Unk.
Senseny, B. R.	60.	Pioche, LC '71-'72.	Unk.
Sharp, R. B.	6g.	Virginia City '71.	Unk.
Shaug, C. W.	16.	Humboldt City, HC '63.	Unk.
Shepherd, J. S.	16.	Santa Clara, PC '63, HC?	Unk.
Sinclair, Clark Bates	7.	EC '97.	Unk/ Independent Med Coll Chicago.
Smart, Joseph Steadman Mullidge	21, 4, 24, 30, 6l, 6m, 6n, 3.	Carson City '77-'81.	New Brunswick, Maine /Bellevue Hosp Med Coll.
Smeathman, H.	24.	HC '64.	Unk.
Smith, A.	1.	Virginia City '60.	Pa/Unk.
Smith, A. Watson	30.	Carson City '79.	Unk/Rush Med Coll.
Smith, E.	68.	Pioche, LC '86 (stayed one month)	Unk.
Smith, Henry J.	23, 4, 40.	WC & Virginia City '85, Wash '90.	Unk/Jefferson Med Coll.
Smith, H. W.	8, 4, 6l, 48 (5.20.77), 49 (10.27.80).	Genoa, DC '75-'80, Supt Schools '78.	Unk/Cleveland Homeo Med Coll.
Smith, U.	6n.	Virginia City '80-'81.	Unk.
Snow, Taylor N.	4, 6k, 6l, 6m, 6n, 40, 69, 70, 71, 72, 73.	Reno '77-'81, Died Baker, Oreg '06.	Ind/Cooper Med Coll.

Snyder, (Nicholas) S.	6k, 38.	Virginia City '77.	Unk/Louisville Med Coll.
Song, William	6h.	Virginia City '72.	Unk.
Southard, Merritt	6f, 27.	Battle Mtn, LaC '83, Austin, LaC '87.	Unk/Bowdin Med Coll, Maine.
Spalding (Spaulding), Volney	23, 6i, 9, 39.	Virginia City '75-'76, Hamilton, WPC '77.	Unk/U City NY
Speer, Hugh Johnstone	23, 4, 6i.	Virginia City '75.	Unk/Harvard Med Coll.
Spencer, Dr.	9.	Virginia City '60.	Unk.
Spinney, H. B.	23, 6i.	Virginia City '75-'76.	Unk/Iowa Med Coll, Keokuk, Iowa.
Spinks, M. A.	63.	Eureka '75.	MS/Unk.
Sponogle, Francis Marion	24, 4, 6l, 6n, 27.	Battle Mtn, LaC '77-'79.	Ohio/Wooster Med Coll, Cleveland, Long Is Coll Hosp, Bellevue Hosp Med Coll.
Sponogle, J. Dorsey	4, 6n, 38	Carlin, Elko '81, Died Seattle, Wash '10.	Unk/Bellevue Hosp Med Coll.
Spruill, J.	39.	New Sante Fe, LC '77.	Unk.
Spurling, S. E. H.	24.	Gold Hill, SC, SC '68.	Unk.
Stackpole, J. S.	25, 8.	WC '60s.	Unk.
Steele (Steel, Steeles), Walcott	22, 21, 6e, 6c, 6h, 6p, 6o, 39, 63, 6a.	Silver City, LyC '64, Winne-mucca, HC pre '65, LaC '75, Dayton, LyC '67, Reno '07, US Army '63, Nev Volunteer (Civil War).	Ohio/Unk.
Steinberger, Carol M.	30.	Carson City '75.	Unk/U Pa.

Stephenson, W. H. C.	9, 21, 6c, 6e, 6p, 6o, 2.	Silver City, LyC '64-, Virginia City '67-'72.	Wash DC/ (Homeo).
Stettinias, James W.	24.	Susanville (Calif), Utah Terr '60.	Unk.
Stevenson, Eady	23, 4, 6k.	Virginia City '75- '77, Wash '82.	Unk/Homeo Med Bd Canada, Cleveland Ho- meo Coll.
Stewart, H. P.	20, 6o.	Pioche, LC '71- '72.	Unk.
Stites, Joseph Angustus	21, 4.	NC '76.	Unk/Bellevue Hosp Med Coll.
Stites, Ida May	27, 46 (unidentified pic- ture).	Battle Mtn, LaC '88.	Unk/Cooper Med Coll.
Stoddard, A. B.,	67.	Virginia City '98.	Unk.
Stoddart, Archibald C.	20, 11, 40.	Elko '77, WC '89.	Unk/Bennett Med Coll Chi- cago: Eclectic Coll Med Surg.
Summers, John Franklin	7, 4.	EC '85,Died Fresno, Calif '25.	Unk/U Calif.
Sussdorff, Gustave E.	30.	Carson City '93.	Unk/Long Is Coll Hosp.
Talcott, L.	6j.	Carson City '73- '74.	Unk.
Taylor, William H.	6h, 6o, 39, 55.	Hamilton, WPC '71-'77, Treasure City, WPC '69.	Unk.
Taylor. William Osborn	23, 4, 6m.	Gold Hill, SC '78-'79, Died Alameda, Calif '04 .	NY/Bellevue Hosp Med Coll.
Temple, W. B.	6o, 39.	Hamilton, WPC '71-'77.	Unk.
Terry, James	23.	Virginia City '75.	Unk/Saint Louis Med Coll.
Terry, Louis	2, 4, 12, 6o, 39.	Elko '70-'77.	La/Montpelier Sch Med, France.

Terry, S.	21, 26, 63.	EuC '75.	La/Cincinnati Literary & Scientific Inst, Physio-Med Coll (Eclectic).
Thiele, Emil	21, 4, 23, 6f, 6j, 6n, 3, 29 (9.22.75).	Virginia City, SC '73-'75, Eureka '80-'81, Hawthorne, MC '87, Died SF, Calif '12.	Russia (Germany)/Amer U (Eclectic) Philadelphia.
Thilido, Francis H.	11.	Elko '98.	Unk/Royal Coll Phy Surg Kingston, C.anada.
Thoma, George H.	21, 9, 4, 25, 6f, 24, 6h, 6l, 6n, 3, 43, 65, 37, 42, (picture), 39, 40, 41, 57.	Austin, LaC '67, Treasure City, WPC '72, Eureka '77-'81, Reno '87, Supt St Hosp '90-'94, Died Reno '07.	NY/Albany Med Coll.
Thomas, C. F.	63, 86	Virginia City, '75-'76.	England/Royal Coll Surg, Eng.
Thomas, C. H.	6o.	Treasuer City, WPC '71-'72.	Unk.
Thomas, George Frederic	23, 4, 6c, 6i, 6k, 40.	Virginia City '64-'77, WC '76, Died Berkeley, Calif '04.	Unk/U Giessen, Germany.
Thomas, W. L.	6f, 6d, 6p.	Austin, LaC '66-'67.	Unk.
Thompson, D. H.	24.	Carson City '77.	Unk.
Thompson, James D.	2, 21, 6e, 6g, 6p, 6o.	Dayton, LyC '68-, Carson City '67-'72.	Ala/Unk.
Thompson, T. C.	39.	Carson City '77.	Unk.
Tierney, E. P.	22.	Winnemucca, HC '75.	Unk.
Tjader, Anton William	2, 21, 6e, 6a, 6b, 6g, 6p, 58, 45, 44.	Washoe City, Carson City '60-'70, Died Carson City '70.	Russia/Harvard Med Coll.
Todd, William	26, 27.	Eureka '80, Battle Mtn, LaC '83.	Unk/Rush Med Coll.

Townsend, Dr.	24.	Nev, date unk.	Unk.
Townsend, Smith J.	43, 64 (Temp lic).	Cherry Ck, WPC '00.	Ill/West Res, U Cleveland.
Tozer, C. H.	29 (7.9.59).	Virginia City '59.	Unk.
Trask, Henry Caustin	9, 4.	Virginia City '82.	Unk/Toland Med Coll.
Trask, Sampson	4, 6n, 27.	Battle Mtn, LaC '79, Austin, LaC '80-'81, Died SF, Calif '20.	Unk/Rector Coll Med, Saint Louis.
True, James	2, 21, 6e, 6m, 3.	Carson City '68-'80.	Vt/Unk.
Tucker, J. C.	9, 6c.	Virginia City SC Hosp '64.	Unk.
Tufford, J. H.	21, 3, 24, 57.	Cherry Creek, WPC '76-'85.	NY/Unk.
Tufts, James E.	21, 23, 6k, 6l, 6m, 6n, 63, 29 (9.22.75).	Virginia City '75-'81.	NY/NY Homeo Med Coll.
Turner, John Franklin	20, 11.	Elko '93.	Unk/U Balto, U West Pa Med Coll.
Underhill, H. J.	21, 6e, 6a, 6c, 6g, 6p.	Virginia City '61-'71.	NY/Unk.
Van Harlingen, Katherine (married name, Fee)	40, 46 (picture), 59.	WC '89-'00.	Ohio/Cooper Med Coll.
Van Zandt, John W.	9, 21, 24, 4, 8, 6k, 6l, 6m, 25.	Virginia City '74-'79, Pres NSMS '75.	Unk/Columbia U Coll Phy Surg.
Voight, Carl B. F.	9, 23, , 6c, 6i, 6m, 6p.	Virginia City '65-'79.	Unk/U Berlin, Paris, Vienna.
Vrooman, M.	6p, 58.	Washoe City '65-'67.	Unk.
Wagner, Henry	23, 4, 6l, 6m, 6n.	Virginia City '76-'81, Died Denver, Colo '19.	Unk/Bellevue Hosp Med Coll.
Wagner, Philippine	21, 4, 64.	Carson City '99, BME '99, Died Carson City '15.	Unk/ Hahnemann Hosp Coll, SF, Calif (Homeo).

Name		Location	Education
Waggoner, Fiedon R.	6n, 40, 3, 61.	Wadsworth, WC '80-'81.	Ill/Wisc Med Coll.
Walker, John	6c.	Virginia City '64.	Unk.
Walley, D.	6p.	Hot Springs, DC '67.	Unk.
Walter, Dr.	24.	Hot Creek, NC '67.	Unk.
Wanson, John	6i.	Gold Hill, SC '74.	Unk.
Warren, William T. C.	40.	WC '97.	Unk/Wisc Eclectic Med Coll.
Waters, John W.	2, 21, 25, 6e, 8, 6k, 24, 65, 6h, 6j, 6i, 6l, 6m, 6o.	Genoa, DC '68, Carson City '71-'79.	Md/Toland Med Coll.
Watkins, C.	6o.	Twin River, NC '71-'72.	Unk.
Watkins, John C.	16.	Winnemucca, HC '70.	Unk.
Watts, S. T.	6p.	Virginia City '67.	Unk.
Wayman John Hudson (With Tjader)	6a, 44.	Carson City '61-'62.	Unk.
Webber, N. Robert	9, 21, 6e, 6f, 6a, 6g, 6h, 6j, 6k, 6p, 6o, 2, 39, 57.	Gold Hill, SC '61-'68, Treasure City, WPC '69, Virginia City'71-'87, Died San Jose, Calif '94.	Va/Unk.
Weed, A. Gideon	21, 24, 25, 8, 6p, 58.	Washoe City '60-'67.	Unk.
Weisich, Elmer Williams	27.	Battle Mtn, LaC '93.	Unk/ Hahnemann Hosp Coll, SF, Calif (Homeo).
Weissenberge, D. F.	63.	SC '75.	Austria/Unk.
Weyland, Issac S.	20, 11.	Elko '85.	Unk/U Pa.
Whipley, D. H.	68.	Pioche, LC '72.	Unk.

White, D. B.	2.	Elko '70.	NY/Unk.
White, Franklin J. (G)	21, 25, 24, 6j, 30, 6l, 65, 6m, 6n, 3, 6f, 6k.	Carson City '70 & Elko, Carson City '75-'81, Virginia City '73-'74, Died San Raphael, Calif '93.	Va/Unk.
White, F. T.	39.	Virginia City '77.	Unk.
White, I.	20, 6o.	Elko '71-'72.	Unk.
White, J.	6p.	Star City, PC '67.	Unk.
White, T.	39.	Elko '77.	Unk.
Wiber, C. E.	57.	WPC '96.	Unk.
Wiggs, J. J.	21, 4.	Elko '70.	Vt/(Allopath).
Wilber, Dr.	57.	WPC ''96.	Unk.
Wild, E. A.	39.	Austin, LaC '77.	Unk/(Homeo).
Wilder, Annie	23, 40.	WC & Virginia City '94.	Unk/Kansas City Coll Med.
Wiles, D. W.	57.	WPC '00.	Unk.
Willard, E. X .	6f, 6d, 6h, 6p, 3, 57.	Austin, LaC '66-'67, Eureka '72, Hamilton, WPC '80-'85.	Mass/Unk.
Willard, E. H.	39.	Shermantown, WPC '77.	Unk.
Willard, Emory L.	6o, 39, 57.	Shermantown, WPC '69-'77.	Unk.
Williams, George Walter	40.	WC '92.	Unk/ Long Is Coll Hosp.
Williams, George Wilson	6f. 52 (5.21.93), Birth Cert (10.6.87).	Genoa, DC '86-'93, DC Co Phy '88.	Unk/Cooper Med Coll (Phy, druggist).
Williams, James	21, 6f, 6l, 6n, 26, 3, 63.	Eureka '75-'81.	NY/Jefferson Med Coll.

Williams, James Albert	4, 30, 40.	WC & Carson City '95.	Unk/Bellevue Hosp Med Coll.
Williams, Leavitt J.	8, 25.	Nev '72.	Unk.
Williams, Lucas Richards	23, 30.	Virginia City '78.	Unk/Rush Med Coll, Chicago.
Williamson, L. Jonathan	21, 60, 2.	Shermantown, WPC '70-'72.	Ohio/Unk.
Willson, W. B.	3.	Candelaria, MC '80.	Ohio/Unk.
Winiham, W. P. L.	8.	Washoe '60s.	Unk.
Wingurd, Edward P.	23.	Virginia City '92.	Unk/Coll Georgio Politam.
Witherspoon, Dr.	17.	Austin, LC '65.	Unk.
Wixon, W. W.	2, 21, 17, 5, 6d, 6l, 6p, 39.	Austin, LC '65-'78.	NY/Unk.
Young, Malon W.	21, 10, 52 (11.18.92), 64, 54 (6.6.79)	Genoa, DC '79-99, DC Co Phy '87-'99.	Unk/Iowa Med Coll, Keokuk, Iowa.
Young, M. G.	6f.	Genoa, DC '87.	Unk.
Zabriskie, C. B.	6a, 6g, 6j, 6i, 6l, 2, 6k, 6m, 6n, 6p, 6o, 61.	Silver City, LyC '61-'81, Gold Hill, SC '71-'72.	NY/Unk.
Zangerlé, John B.	9, 4, 6f, 23, 6k, 6l, 6m, 6n.	Virginia City '77-'90, Died '90.	Unk/ Long Is Coll Hosp.

[1] The dates recorded on this chart only indicate when these individuals were in the territory or in Nevada. They do not necessarily indicate when a doctor came or left, and what is just as important, in many instances there is little or no evidence that they practiced medicine. Furthermore, in some cases there is no definite evidence that those listed were physicians, only that they were called doctor. Obviously the more resources listed increases the evidence that the individual was a physician and practiced medicine. The abbreviation for a state are accepted standard abbreviations. Other abbreviations are: BME = Board of Medical Examiners; Bro = brother; CMA = California Medical Association; Coll = College; Ed = editor; ENT = Ear, Nose and Throat; Homeo = Homeopathy; Illeg = illegible; Is = Island; NSMS = Nevada State Medical Society, Off = officer; Pyr = Pyramid; Temp lic = Temporary license; Terr = Territory; Unk = unknown; U = University; UCSF = Univ. Calif. San Francisco; EC = Esmeralda County; ElC = Elko County; LC = Lincoln County; SC = Storey County; WC = Washoe County; LaC = Lander County; Lyon County = LyC; WPC = White Pine County; HC = Humboldt County; OC = Ormsby County; DC = Douglas County; MC = Mineral County; NC = Nye County; CC = Churchill County; EuC = Eureka County; and PC = Pershing County. Sources are listed in Appendix V.

[2] Some physicians in 1899 refused to pay for their license and their records may not be present in the BME files.

19th-Century Women Doctors[1]

Name	Source	City/Co & Date	Born/ Education
Albers, Annet	43.	Washoe '00.	Germany/ Unk.
Andersen, Helen	6m, 3.	Reno '78-'79, Carson City '80.	Denmark/ Unk.
Atwater, Hattie F.	4, 30.	Carson City '82.	Unk/Wooster Med Coll, Cleveland.
Buchins, A. C. (Doctress)	21, 63.	Elko '75.	La/Unk.
Clark, Elizabeth	3, 82, 83 (Fall '73).	Ward, WPC '80.	Unk/(Homeo).
Cook, Eliza	21, 10, 19 (picture), 43, 46 (picture).	Sheridan, DC '99, Prob '84, Died 10.2.47.	Utah/Cooper Med Coll.
De Forrest, Brown	6n.	Virginia City '80-'81.	Unk.
DeLong, C. E.	21, 63.	HC '75.	La/Unk.
Fee, Katherine (maiden name, VanHarlingen)	4, 21, 59.	WC '89-'00.	Ohio/Cooper Med Coll.
Geiss, Anna	40.	WC '89.	Unk/Cohner Med Coll, Alsace, Germany.
Grey, Georgia (Mrs. W. S.)	6f, 3, 57.	Hamilton, WPC '80-'87.	Unk.
Hastings, Carrie B. Flower	23, 4.	Virginia City '92, Died Sedalia, Mo.	Unk/Kansas City Hosp Coll Med.

Hoffman, Doctress	29 (4.12.65), 86.	Virginia City '65.	Unk/Educated in Germany.
Jones, Helena (Doctress and Accoucheur)	21, 6o, 39, 57.	Treasure City, WPC '69-'77.	Denmark/ Unk.
Longshore-Potts, Anna Mary	23, 4.	Virginia City '97, Died San Diego '12.	Unk/Women's Med Coll Pa.
McGarver, (Mary)	43.	Golconda, HC '00.	Pa/Unk.
Newland, Ruth E.	23, 4.	Virginia City '82.	Unk/Med Eclectic Coll Cincinnati.
Post-Van Orden, Catherine Nicholas	23, 6n, 46 (picture).	Virginia City '79-'81.	Unk/Cooper Med Coll.
Seals, Ramlis	3.	Ward, WPC '80.	Ill/Unk.
Stites, Ida May	27, 46 (unidentified picture).	Battle Mtn, LaC '88.	Unk/Cooper Med Coll.
Van Harlingen, Katherine (married name, Fee)	40, 46 (picture), 59.	WC '89-'00.	Ohio/Cooper Med Coll.
Wilder, Annie	23, 40.	WC & Virginia City '94.	Unk/Kansas City Coll Med.

---

[1] Sources are listed in Appendix V.

APPENDIX III

19th-Century Chinese Doctors¹

Name	Source	City/Co - Date	Education/ Title
Ack Sue Tong	3.	Eureka '80.	Chinese physician.
Ah Gung	3.	Eureka '80.	Chinese physician.
Ah Hung	2.	Virginia City '70.	Chinese doctor.
Ah Jet	3.	Tuscarora, ElC '80.	Chinese doctor.
Ah Kee	6g, 2.	Carson City '70-'79.	Botanical doctor, Chinese physician.
Ah Lang	2.	Virginia City '70.	Chinese physician
Ah Lee	2.	Elko '70.	Chinese physician.
Ah Quang	2.	OC '70.	Chinese doctor.
Ah Sam	2.	HC '70.	Chinese physician.
Ah Sid	3.	Wadsworth, WC '80.	Chinese doctor.
Ah Tong	39.	Carson City '77.	Chinese physician.
Ah Wah	2.	WC '70.	Chinese physician.
Ah Wang	3.	WPC '80.	Chinese doctor.
Ah Yo	63.	EuC '75.	Chinese physician.
Che Chung Hing	3.	Reno '80.	Chinese physician.

Chin Guy	3.	Reno '80.	Chinese physician.
Chin Pooty	6m.	Virginia City '78–'79.	Chinese physician.
Chow E	3.	Spring Valley Indian Township, WPC '80.	Unk.
Coke Sung	6m.	Virginia City '78–'79.	Chinese physician.
Gim Hin	6j.	Virginia City '73–'79.	Chinese physician.
Hing Ho	23 (medical certificate).	Virginia City '86.	Hong Hong Apprenticeship.
Hing T. Wah	40.	WC '90.	Doy Yak Tong, Canton.
Hop Lock	62.	Virginia City '60s–'70.	Chinese doctor.
Hop Lop	6j.	Virginia City '73.	Unk.
Hop Wing	29 (9.22.75).	Virginia City '75.	Chinese physician.
Hope See	2.	OC '70.	Chinese doctor.
Hy Yick Chew	62.	Tybo, NC '77.	Chinese physician.
Jem Kee	6m.	Gold Hill, SC '78.	Chinese physician.
Jim Hei	3.	Virginia City '80.	Chinese doctor.
Kee Carfung	3.	Carson City '80.	Chinese physician.
Kee Chung	43.	Candelaria, MC.	Chinese physician.
Kee Lock	3.	Carson City '80.	Chinese doctor.
Ken Fung	20.	Elko '73–'76.	Sch Med & Surg Canton.
Lee Lo	2.	OC '70.	Chinese doctor.
Leing Shee Cheng	2.	WC '70.	Unk.
Long Yut	20.	Elko '76.	Sch Med & Surg Canton.

Men Lee	3.	Eureka '80.	Chinese physician.
Mong Ho	3.	Carson City '80.	Chinese physician.
Nung Kee	3.	Eureka '80.	Chinese physician.
On Kee	39.	Virginia City '77.	Chinese physician.
Ou	3.	Carson City '80.	Chinese physician.
Qort (Illeg) Ahi	2.	OC '70.	Chinese doctor.
Quong Shang	6m.	Virginia City '78-'79.	Chinese physician.
Quy Fong	6g.	Virginia City '71.	Chinese physician.
Quy Fung	68.	Pioche, LC '73	Chinese physician.
Sing Tong Loo	2.	Virginia City '70.	Chinese physician.
Song Wing	2.	Virginia City '70.	Chinese doctor.
Tanig On Gek	2.	WC '70.	Unk.
Tong Lee	2, 63.	WC '70-'75.	Unk.
Tong Sing Tung	2.	OC '70.	Chinese doctor.
U. Wing Shang	23.	Virginia City '78.	Harbor Dept Hong Kong.
Wa Sang	57.	WPC '85-'89.	Unk.
Wai Tong	62 (picture).	Carson City '99-'00.	Herb doctor, Chinese phy.
Wan Gee	3.	Ward, WPC '80.	Chinese doctor.
Wan Quong	2.	OC '70.	Chinese doctor.
Wing Song	6m.	Virginia City '78-'81.	Chinese physician.
Wo Hing	23.	Virginia City '86.	Hong Kong.
Wong Quong	39.	Reno '77.	Unk.
Yel Sam	3.	Carson City '80.	Chinese doctor.

Yon Haong	6m.	Virginia City '78.	Chinese physician.
Yuch Uh	3.	Tybo, NC '80.	Unk.
Yung Hung	3.	Carson City '80.	Unk.
Yung Lin	3.	Eureka '80.	Chinese physician.

---

[1] Sources are listed in Appendix V.

APPENDIX IV

Early Midwives[1]

Name	Source	City/Co - Date
Abraham, Sarah Corney	77, 79.	Carson City '75.
Aldrich, Mrs.	10.	DC '92.
Anderson, Mrs. Helen	3, 6m.	Reno '78 (physician, midwife).
Armstrong, Mrs. Ben	20.	Star Valley, ElC 1900s.
Ascagorta, Gregoria	80.	Ione, NC early 1900s (medicine woman, doctor, midwife.
Bauman, Martha	80.	Fallon, CC early 1900s.
Bellmere, Julia	6m.	Virginia City '78.
Blackee, Mrs. Fannie	10.	DC '92.
Bradley, Mrs. Bill	82.	WPC late 1800s.
Bull, Mrs.	10.	DC '91.
Cameron, Mrs. Jacob	82.	Spring Valley, PC '70s, '80s.
Christensen, Mrs.	10.	DC '91.
Christensen, Mrs. J.	10.	DC '97.
Clark, Mrs. Elizabeth	3, 82, 66 (Fall '73).	Ward, WPC '80s (homeopath, midwife)
Dakin, Mary "Granny"	20.	Elko early 1900s.
DePoali, Mr. A.	10.	DC '98 (accoucheur).
Dip Lee	Nev. St. Museum	Winnemucca '80s-
Drannan, Mrs. S.M.	6m.	Reno '78.
Ferrin, Emily J.	20.	ElC early 1900s.
Frasier, Hannah Kent	7, 79.	Cherry Creek & Ely, WPC '90.
Frazier, Mrs.	10.	DC''90.

Fredericks, Mrs. E.	10.	DC '97.
Fulton, Mrs. H.	10.	DC '99.
Giardelli, Mrs. Martina	10.	DC 1912.
Giaudelli, Mrs. M.	10.	DC '95.
Gray. Mrs. Annie	10.	DC '87.
Guisti, Virginia Boitano	77, 79.	Cortez & Mt. Tenabo, EuC early 1900s.
Hawkins, Mrs.	10.	DC '91, '97.
Hawkins, Mrs. G.W.	10.	DC '97, '98.
Hignirra, Ambrosia	20.	Tuscarora, ElC early 1900s.
Hoffman, Doctress	29, 86.	Virginia City '65
Huber, Christina	Great grand-daughter Helen Oster	Mountain City 'late 1800s.
Jepsen, Mrs. H.	10.	DC '02.
Jessen, Mrs.	10.	DC''89.
Jessen, Mrs. Henriette	10.	DC '98.
Jones, Mrs. Tom	20.	Elko early 1900s.
Kleckner, Mrs. Viola	20.	Independence Valley, ElC early 1900s.
Klotz, Mrs. F.	10.	DC '97.
Knoff, Mrs. Annie	11.	Elko early 1900s.
Leberski, Mrs. Francis	11.	ElC early 1900s.
Litton, Mrs. G.W.	11.	Elko early 1900s.
Mabel Baker ?	81.	Mountain City, ElC early 1900s.
Moiola, Mrs.	80.	Fallon, CC early 1900s.
Mulvaney, Mrs.	80.	Fallon, CC early 1900s.
Neddenreip, Mrs. F.	10.	DC '97.
Neddenriep, Anna Mueller Engel	83.	Carson Valley, OC late 1800s.
O'Brien, Mrs. Jane	11.	Starr Valley, ElC early 1900s.
Oglivie, Mrs. Jane	11.	South Fork, ElC early 1900s.

Oxborrow, Mary Leicht	77, 79, 82.	Lund, WPC early 1900s.
Penaise, Mrs.	10.	DC '97.
Reboule, Mrs. A.	11.	Lamoille, ElC early 1900s.
Rich, Mariah Berdilla	84.	Panaca, LC '91.
Roach, Tillie (Mrs. Amos)	20.	Elko early 1900s.
Robinson, Mrs.	10.	DC '91.
Scott, Doctress Alace	3.	Belleville, EC '80.
Scott, Mrs.	82.	Osceola, WPC '80s.
Simonsen, Miss Ella	81.	Elko early 1900s (had maternity home)
Smith, Mr. J.H.	10.	DC '97.
Smith, Mrs.	10.	DC '98.
Stancil, Mr. Henry	10.	DC 1902 (accoucheur).
Staples, A. C.	57.	WPC '82.
Swallow, Anna Day	82.	Shoshone area, WPC '90s.
Thorpe, Mrs. Margaret	11.	Elko early 1900s.
VanElten, Mrs.	10.	DC '99.
Vasquez, Nora	80.	Fallon, CC early 1900s.
Waldorf, Mrs.	10.	DC '97.
Whitaker, Mr. O. (or A.) B.	10.	DC '98 (accoucheur).
Williams, Mrs. J.	10.	DC '98.
Wilslef, Mrs. Emma C.	10.	DC '06.
Windous, Margaret Christina Arnoldus	77, 79, 82.	White River & Ely, WPC 1908.
Wines, Mrs. Naomi	20.	Ruby Valley, ElC early 1900s.
Young, Mrs. Mary	6a.	Virginia City '62.

---

[1] Names listed in Appendix IV indicate those people whose profession as midwife has been either proven or suggested by documents such as birth certificates filed in county offices or the memories of current residents of Nevada. This is, by necessity, only a partial list of the people who enabled Nevada and the United States to expand in population and wealth. It can be multiplied many times.

APPENDIX V

Sources for Appendices I-IV[1]

1. 1860 U.S. Census.
2. 1870 U.S. Census.
3. 1880 U.S. Census.
4. *Directory of Deceased American Physicians 1804-1929.*
5. Berlin, *Silver Platter.*
6. City Directories of the United States, Segment II, 1861-1881.

    6a. Kelly, *First Directory of Nevada Territory* (1862).

    6b. *Second Directory of Nevada Territory; etc.* (1863).

    6c. *Mercantile Guide and Directory for Virginia City, etc.* (1864-5) and *San Francisco Business Directory and Mercantile Guide* (1864-5).

    6d. *Harrington's Directory of the City of Austin* (1866).

    6e. *The Nevada Directory* (1868-1869).

    6f. *McKenney's Pacific Coast Directory* 1886-1887.

    6g. *Storey, Ormsby, Washoe & Lyon Counties Directory* (1871-1872).

    6h. *McKenney's Gazetteer & Directory of the Central Pacific RR,* 1872.

    6i. *General Business and Mining Directory of Storey, etc.,* 1875.

6j. *Virginia and Truckee Railroad Directory* **1873-74.**

6k. *Business Directory of San Francisco and Principal Towns etc.* **1877.**

6l. *Business Directory of the Pacific States and Territories* **1878.**

6m. *Bishop's Directory of Virginia City etc.* **1878-9.**

6n. *Pacific Coast Directory* **1880-1881.**

6o. *Pacific Coast Directory* **1871-1872.**

6p. *Pacific Coast Directory* **1867.**

7. Esmeralda County Recorder's ledgers.

8. Davis, *The History of Nevada.*

9. *Doten, The Journals of Alfred.*

10. Douglas County Recorder's ledgers.

11. Elko County Recorder's ledgers.

12. *Elko Chronicle.*

13. *Elko Independent.*

14. Hyatt, *Frontier Times.*

15. Humboldt County Recorder's ledgers.

16. *Humboldt Register.*

17. Lewis, *Martha and the Doctor.*

18. Lincoln County Recorder's ledgers.

19. *Nevada State Journal.*

20. Patterson, *Sagebrush Doctors and ....*

21. Ross' *Directory of Nevada Physicians.*

22. *Silver State.*

23. Storey County Recorder's ledgers.

24. Angel, Myron, *History of Nevada.*

25. Walker, *Story of the Nev. State Soc. and Nev. Med.*

26. Eureka County Recorder's ledgers.

27. Lander County Recorder's ledgers.

28. Nye County Recorder's ledgers.

29. *Territorial Enterprise.*

30. Orsmby (Carson City) County Recorder's ledgers.

31. Stewart, *Adolph Sutro.*

32. Daniels, *Life and Death of Julia Bulette.*

33. *NE Nev. Hist. Soc. Quart.*

34. White Pine County Recorder's ledgers.

35. Lyon County Recorder's ledgers.

36. Esmeralda County (Lyon County Office).

37. Wren, *A History of the State of Nevada.*

38. *American Medical Directory 1906.*

39. Butler, *Medical Register and Directory of the United States, 1877.*

40. Washoe County Recorder's ledgers.

41. Washoe County Med. Soc. and Nev. St. Med. Assoc. Records.

42. Scrugham, *Nevada*

43. 1900 U.S. Census.

44. Wayman, *A Doctor on the California Trail.*

45. Cerveri, *With Curry's Compliments.*

46. Stanford Univ. Lane Med. Lib., Spec. Collect.

47. Ashbaugh, *Nevada's Turbulent Yesterday.*

48. *News.*

49. *Genoa Journal.*

50. *Douglas County Banner.*

51. *Record-Courier.*

52. *Genoa Weekly Courier.*

53. Douglas County Tax List.

54. *Carson Valley News.*

55. Mitchell Papers, Huntington Lib.

56. *Notable American Women.*

57. *White Pine News.*

58. Ratay, *Boom Times in Old Washoe City.*

59. *Reno Evening Gazette.*

60. Lewis, *Silver Kings.*

61. Jones, *Memories, Men and Medicine.*

62. Geiger, *Trail to California.*

62. Nev. State Museum, Carson City.

63. 1875 Nev. Census.

64. Nev. Bd. Med. Examiners records.

65. Walker, *A Life's Review and Notes....*

66. *Nev. Hist. Soc. Quart.*

67. Letter to Senator W.W. Stewart, February 4, 1898.

68. *Pioche Weekly Record.*

69. *Centennial History of Oregon 1811-1912.*

70. *Illustrated History of Baker, Grant, Malheur and Harney Counties.*

71. *The Story of Oregon.*

72. Hines, *Illustrated History of the State Oregon.*

73. Larsell, *The Doctor in Oregon.*

74. Reifschneider, *Nev. Highways & Parks.*

75. Univ. Nev. Getchell Lib., Spec. Collect.

76. Univ. Calif. Bancroft Lib.

77. A.A.U.W., *Pioneer Women of Nevada.*

78. *White Pine County Early Nev. Families.*

79. *Ormsby County Early Nev. Families,.* Interview with Marion LaVoy.

81. Interview with Marie Thompson.

82. Read, *White Pine Lang Syne.*

83. Paher, *Nevada Towns and Tales.*

84. Lingenfelter, *The Hardrock Miners.*

85. Winchell, *History of Fresno County....*

86. Goldman, *Gold Diggers and Silver Miners.*

---

[1] For complete listing of the sources see bibliography.

Simeon L. Lee Letter to the U. S. Surgeon-General

8/19/01

Dear Doctor:

I send you by registered mail, under a separate cover, the blank you sent me with the information desired, also a photograph.

I may, and doubtless will seem strange to you that one who took his degree from an irregular school should be so generally recognized as I am in this state, and I seem called upon, as it were, to explain the.... I was a lad, comparatively when I matriculated in the school from which my father's family physician graduated. Of course I then thought it the only college. I have, I think, grown wiser since.

I now know no pathy... or [isue], but endeavor to master the mysteries which constantly confronts the physician so far as all ordinary mentality enables me to do.

I have fought the fight for the third of a century, have kept the faith and never debased the high calling of the true healer nor soiled the professional [evcise...].

I am secretary of both our State Boards; That of Health and Registration and Examination, a position given me by the votes of my associates, all of whom save one are regulars.

In addition to the information given you, I may state that I am the Medical Examiner for 13 old line or fraternal Insurance Companies headed by the Mutual Life of NY.

That for ten years there was never a Capital operation performed in this city. I am by myself and yet we always have from six to ten physicians and surgeons.

Believe me, Doctor, I do not write this in a spirit of egotisiek [sic], but simply to explain why I have been so favored not only by the Governors of this state, but by the profession.

My baby son is now a senior in the medical Dept. of the university of California and next May I shall send him to London and Paris to finish his student work.

Believe Me, Truly yours [signed S. L. Lee]

E. A. Grosh Letter to his Father

Gold Canõn, Sept. 7th 1857[1]

Dear Father.—

I take up my pen with a heavy heart, for I have sad news to send you. God has seen fit in his perfect wisdom & goodness to call Hosea, the patient, the good, the gentle to join his Mother in another & a better world than this....

At the time of his death I had gone to see a physician in Eagle Valley, some 14 or 15 miles from here. It was very sudden—unexpected but very peaceful. Not a shudder, not a gasp, not a change of feature marked the parting of soul and body. He simply fell asleep. It was such a death as God blesses the good with.

The immediate cause of his death was the wound in the foot I mentioned in my last. It occurred about the middle of the forenoon of Wednesday, Aug. 19th, [by first letter] or Thursday the 20th. He died Wednesday, Sept. 2d. We were packing dirt from a small ravine to the right fork of the main Canõn. I dug and Hosea drove the jack.

We had brought no water with us, for drinking and becoming thirsty (it was very hot) I started down to the main ravine for a drink. I met Hosea as he was coming back for another load and told him what I was going for and that I had not quite a load dug for him. On my return he was setting on the ground beside the dirt holding his left foot in his hand. "I have done it now," he shouted as I came within hearing, and on my asking what he had done, he said that he had "struck the pick into his foot" "Why how in the world did you do it" I asked as I first saw the wound. It was a frightful gash. The dirt we were digging was only 16 or 18 inches deep, and, though it dug hard, there were but few stones in it. He smiled, and said that he hardly knew how he did it. He then pointed to a large quartz rock laying loose on top of the ground just on the edge of the hole. "Somehow" he said "I hit that." He would not let me carry him to the house but rode the jack. The ground was rough, and the jolting caused him considerable pain.

For about a week it got on finely, in spite of the hot weather. But the evening of the eighth day, his foot was swolen [sic], & the wound was closed. The next morning I lanced the foot in two places and got out considerable matter, which relieved the pain, and checked the swelling. I also changed the poultice from rosin soap to bread & soda. The bread & soda worked very well, and I think that if we had continued it everything would have come out right. In all matters concerning sickness I generally deferred to his opinion. He thought if we only could get Indian-meal to substitute for the bread it would get along faster. On going down to the store I found a pound or two of old indian-meal. It was about half bran. That night we tried a poultice of it. The next morning I did not like the look of it and asked him if I had not better go back to the bread again. I thought the bran was too healing. He answered, "Let us try once more and see how that works, I was very feverish all last night, and maybe that is all that is the matter with it" In about two hours, he complained of a strange sensation in the foot. He said that it seemed as if a little ball was underneath the flesh and was running all over his foot. On examining the poultice was dry & the wound was closed. Though we tried the bread & soda again we could not get it to draw right. That night he suffered much pain. From this on I gave up all idea of working though we had not a cent and were in debt. I might have done so before just as well, for my time was so broken up by loss of sleep, etc. that it amounted to nothing.

Monday afternoon I went down to the store—four or five miles—to see if I could get either opium or laudanum, so that he might get his necessary rest. I could find neither But I saw Mr. Rose, and he told me that he had some at his house in

Eagle Valley. He also recommended me to try fresh
cow=dung as a poultice. I took some cow=dung up
with me, and applied it immediately. I should have
mentioned that the leg had commenced swelling,
and that we could not check it. The poultice at once
checked the swelling, and ...ed the pain, and next
morning everything was looking well again. I
found a man who was going up to Eagle Valley and
sent by him for the opium, and also for a little quinine cayenne & several other things if they could be
got. I could get nothing here & Hosea was quite bil-
lious [sic] besides touched with the dyspepsia—the
result of his confinement to bed. I understood the
man would be back that evening, but that evening
found that I was mistaken. This evening also
occurred the misshap [sic] which I think sent Hosea
out of this world. The cat jumped on the bed, and
in doing so lit with all his weight on poor Hosea's
sore foot. It cause him intense pain. That night he
suffered great pain, and next morning he had a
high nervous fever, accompanied with ... complained that during the night he had been slightly
flighty. He was very cool & calm, and before I went
to see Dr. King (formerly of Dearfield N.Y.) & with
whom we had some slight aquaintance [sic] we had
considerable conversation, He [Hosea] said, that
"through God's mercy we had passed through as
great trials as this—and to that mercy we must
trust—without God's mercy what would we be?

Dear Brother! he spoke as though the trial was as much on me as on him. He was so uncomplaining & made so little of his sufferings that it took close watching to see how sick he really was. After some little thought he consented to a proposition I made to send to you for $50. or $100. so that we could, on the strength of it secure the services of Dr. Daggert [Dr. Charles Daggett], the only good DOCTOR in Carson Valley, should they be necessary. Little did either of us dream of the danger being so near at hand.

I dressed his foot. It was rather cold. He quieted my apprehentions [sic] by saying that it was the effect of the warm poultices. The poultice was warmer, a little, than blood heat. He felt it very sensible, and we both congratulated ourselves on the favorable symptom, as the poultice before that had been warmer and he had hardly felt it. He complained of being ... sick", just before I left, but felt no other pain.

About 9 A.M. I started for Eagle Valley to see Dr. King and get what medicine I could, leaving him in charge of Mr. Galphins, who came to the house a few minutes after I had left. I had not gone far before a feeling of uneasiness took hold of me. Twice I threw myself down behind a cedar bush, completely overcome with a great dread that it would terminate fatally. I prayed—oh with what agony I prayed that he be spared—that the loss of

the limb might be the worst. Finally to get rid of
this dreadful apprehension I struck across the
mountains, which though it shortened the distance
a few miles, was very rough, and I was almost bare-
footed. Dr. King was very kind to me. He recommended the continunance [sic] of the cow dung
poultice, as being the best to be had here. He did not
regard the swelling of the foot & leg—neither the
coldness—as anything serious. He spoke spoke [sic]
as if a wound got along very slow in this country,
but did not seem to think that the danger was
increased thusly. Hosea complained of pain in the
back, and one particular spot, near the shoulders on
the left side, he said produced nausea if it touched
the bed the doctor regarded it only as the result of
the pain & loss of sleep together with slight bil-
liousness [sic] He gave me four pills of Blue Mass—
which I took for fear of hurting his feelings. But I
got ten or fifteen grains of quinine.

[2nd sheet]

Though I could get no physic but aloes or Ep.
Salts, both of which we had and would not use. I
regretted very much that I could get no hops, as I
had more hope of allaying the nausea with that
than anything I could think of. Of Mrs. Rose I got
some Opium & a few ounces of garden peppers. I
started back with a lightened heart. It was just dark
as I got back. Mr. Galphin met me a few steps from

the house. "You must prepare yourself for bad news, Allen" he said. I heard strange voices in the cabin, and I thought that either Dr. Daggert [Daggett], or some physician travelling across the plains had come on to the Canōn & had been sent up by the miners below, (as Hosea was thought a great deal of) and that it might have been pronounced necessary to amputate the foot. I was quite unprepared for the answer to my "what it is?" "Hosea is dead!" Oh the terrible force of that blow! Oh! the utter desolation of that hour....

When I left I forgot to get some peppermint tea I had made for him, within his reach. He was getting up for it as Mr. Galphin came in, who told him to lie still, & handed it to him. He drank pretty heartily of it, and in a few minutes threw it up. Mr. G. then heated some water at his request, and gave him a couple of spoonfuls, which remained on the stomach. About 2 hours after he had occasion to get up and Mr. G. helped him, he complained much of nausea and weakness, He had sunk very much since I had left. He said as he lay down "this country doesn't suit me" and Mr. G. thinks he added "and I am going to leave it" Mr. G. thought that it was best for him not to talk, He therefore walked into the other room, and laid down on he bed, so that he could see him Hosea remained perfectly quiet for some time, and Mr. G. thinks that he was asleep. An hour or more he heard Hosea breath hard &

went to him, & spoke to him. Hosea heard him, for he partially turned his head to him, and opened his eyes, but did not fix him. His eyes closed again as if he had fallen asleep. His breath shortened easily and without effort, - "it died away" to use Mr. Galphin's expression. His features wore an expression of happy pleasant, sleep, and with his last breath he did not even stretch himself. "he fell asleep". Let us thank our Heavenly Father, for even as he envelopes us in a cloud of sorrow his mercy shines through it....

Truly and Affectionately your son [signed E. A. Grosh]

---

[1] The original letter is in possession of Charles T. Wegman of Bloomfield, New Jersey. A typed copy, sent to Mr. Eric Moody of the Nevada Historical Society, was used by the author. Mr. Wegman reviewed the manuscript as transcribed in Appendix VI and approved its use, and made corrections to Mr. Moody's copy after consulting the original letter.

Bibliography

Books and Directories

American Medical Directory 1906 (Chicago: Amer. Med. Assoc., 1906)

Angel, Myron, ed., *History of Nevada with Illustrations and Biographical Sketches of its Prominent Men and Pioneers* (Oakland, Calif.: Thompson & West, 1881) reissued by (Berkeley: Howell-North, 1958) Poulson, Helen J., *Index to Thompson and West's History of Nevada*, Bibliographical Series, no. 6 (Reno: Univ. Nev. Press, 1966).

Armstrong, Robert D., *A Preliminary Union Catalog of Nevada Manuscripts* (Reno: Univ. Nev. Lib., 1967).

Ashbaugh, Don, *Nevada's Turbulent Yesterday: a Study in Ghost Towns* (Las Vegas: Westernlore Press, 1963).

Austin, Mary, foreword, *Doctor Nellie* (Mammoth Lakes, Calif.: Genny Smith Books, 1983).

Barlow, Jeffrey, and Christine Richardson, *China Doctor of John Day* (Portland, Ore.: Binford & Mort, 1979).

Berlin, Ellin, *Silver Platter* (Garden City, N.Y.: Doubleday & Co., 1957).

Biennial Report of the Commissioners and Superintendent, *Indigent Insane of Nevada* (Carson City: 1883-1902).

Burton, Richard F., *The City of the Saints, and Across the Rocky Mountains to California* (N.Y.: Harper & Bros., 1862).

Butler, Samuel W., *The Medical Register and Directory of the United States* (Phila.: Off. Med. Surg. Reporter, 1877).

California Medical Directory, 1878.

Carlson, Helen S., *Nevada Place Names: A Geographical Dictionary* (Reno: Univ. Nev. Press, 1974).

Centennial History of Oregon 1811-1912, 2 vols. (Chicago: S. J. Clarke Pub. Co., 1912).

City Directories of the United States, Segment II, 1861-1881.

    Bishop's Directory of Virginia City etc. 1878-9 (San Francisco: 1878).

    Business Directory of the Pacific States and Territories for 1878 (San Francisco: 1878).

    Business Directory of San Francisco and Principal Towns of California and Nevada, 1877 (San Francisco: 1877).

    Collins, Charles, *Mercantile Guide and Directory for Virginia City, Gold Hill, Silver City and American City, etc.* (Virginia City: 1864-5).

    General Business and Mining Directory of Storey, etc., 1875.

    Gillis, William, *Nevada Directory, for 1868-69* (Virginia City: 1868).

    Harrington's Directory of the City of Austin 1866 by Myron Angel (Austin, Nev.: J. D. Fairchild Co., 1866).

    Kelly, J. Wells, *First Directory of Nevada Territory, etc.* (San Francisco: 1862).

    Langley, Henry G., *Pacific Coast Directory for 1867: etc.*

    Langley, Henry G., *Pacific Coast Directory for 1871-72* (San Francisco: 1871).

    McKenney's Gazetteer & Directory of the Central Pacific Railroad for 1871 (Sacramento).

McKenney's Gazetteer & Directory of the Central Pacific Railroad, 1872.

McKenney's Pacific Coast Directory 1886-1887 (San Francisco: L. M. McKenney & Co., 1886).

Pacific Coast Directory for 1880-1881 (San Francisco: 1880).

Second Directory of Nevada Territory; etc. (1863).

Stilwell, B.F., *San Francisco Business Directory and Mercantile Guide for 1864* (San Francisco: B.F. Stilwell & Co., 1864).

Storey, Ormsby, Washoe & Lyon Co. Directory (1871-2).

Uhlhorn, John F., *Virginia and Truckee Railroad Directory 1873-74* (Sacramento: 1873).

Coe, Urling C., *Frontier Doctor* (N.Y.: Macmillan Co., 1939).

Corbusier, William T., *Verde to San Carlos: Recollections of a Famous Army Surgeon and His Observant Family on the Western Frontier, 1869-1886* (Tucson: Dale S. King, 1969).

Cragen, Dorothy Clora, *The Boys in the Sky-Blue Pants: The Men and Events at Camp Independence and Forts of Eastern California, Nevada and Utah, 1862-1877* (Fresno: Pioneer Pub. Co., 1975).

Daniels, Zeke (Effie Mona Mack?) *The Life and Death of Julia C. Bulette, "Queen of the Red Lights"* (Virginia City: Lamp Post, 1958).

Davis, Sam P., ed., *The History of Nevada*, 2 vols. (Reno: Elms Pub. Co., 1913).

Dawson, Alson W. and Lillian, *Greener Grass* (Boise: Dawson House, 1984).

D'Azevedo, Warren L., *Great Basin, Handbook of North American Indians*, vol. 11 (Wash., D.C.: Smithsonian , 1986).

De Quille, Dan, (William Wright) *The Big Bonanza: An Authentic Account of the Discovery,, History, and Working of the World-Renowned Comstock Lode of Nevada...* (N.Y.: Alfred A. Knopf, 1953).

Directory of Deceased American Physicians 1804-1929 (Chicago: Amer. Med. Assn., 1993).

Doetsch, Raymond N., *Journey to the Green and Golden Lands: The Epic of Survival on the Wagon Trail* (Port Washington, N.Y.: National Univ. Pub., 1976)

Doten, Alfred, *Journals of Alfred Doten, 1849-1903*, 3 vols., Walter V. T. Clark, ed. (Reno: Univ. Nev. Press, 1973).

Drake, Daniel, *A Systematic Treatise, Historical, Etiological, and Practical on the Principal Diseases of the Interior Valley of North America, as They Appear in the ...*, 2 vols. (Cincinnati: Winthrop B. Smith & Co., 1850).

Drury, Wells, *An Editor on the Comstock Lode* (Palo Alto: Pacific Books, 1948).

Duffy, John, *Epidemics in Colonial America* (Baton Rouge: State Univ. Press, 1953).

_____, *The Healers: The Rise of the Medical Establishment* (N.Y.: McGraw-Hill, 1976).

Dunlop, Richard, *Doctors of the American Frontier: A Tribute to the Healing Instinct of the Early American Medicine Men - and to the Stamina of their Patients* (Garden City, N.Y.: Doubleday & Co., 1965).

Elliott, Russell R., *History of Nevada* (Lincoln: Univ. Neb. Press, 1973).

Ellison, Marion, "Angel of Mercy," Stanley W. Paher, ed., *Nevada Towns and Tales*, Vol. 1 (Las Vegas: Nev. Pub., 1981-1982).

Fiero, Bill, *Geology of the Great Basin* (Reno: Univ. Nev. Press, 1986).

Fulton, Robert Lardin, *Epic of the Overland* (San Francisco: A. M. Robertson, 1924).

Garnier, Dr. Pierre, *A Medical Journey in California*, Nunis, Doyce B. Jr., Intro. and annotated, Trans. by L. Jay Oliva (Los Angeles: Zeitlin & Ver Brugge, 1967).

Geiger, Vincent and Wakeman Bryarly, *Trail to California: The Overland Journal of Vincent Geiger and Wakeman Bryarly* (New Haven: Yale Univ. Press, 1945).

Geuder, Patricia, ed., *Pioneer Women of Nevada* (Carson City, Nev.: Delta Kappa Gamma Society, A.A.U.W. Nev. Div., 1976).

Goldman, Marion S., *Gold Diggers and Silver Miners: Prostitution and Social Life on the Comstock Lode* (Ann Arbor: Univ. Mich. Press, 1981).

Gorman, Harry M., *My Memories of the Comstock* (Los Angeles: Suttonhouse Pub., 1939).

Grob, Gerald N., *The Mad Among Us: A History of the Care of America's Mentally Ill* (N.Y.: Free Press, 1994).

Haller, John S., Jr., *Medical Protestants: The Eclectics in American Medicine, 1825-1939* (Carbondale: So. Ill. Univ. Press, 1994).

Harris, Henry, *California's Medical Story* (San Francisco: Grabborn Press, 1932).

Hawthorne, Julian, *The Story of Oregon*, 2 vols. (N.Y.: Amer. Hist. Pub. Co., 1892).

Hiller, Frederick, *Common Sense vs. Allopathic Humbuggery; or, Chloroform* and *Apoplexy Duly Considered in Connection with Certain Allopathic Luminaries* (Virginia City: 1868).

_____, *Medical Truths and Light for the Million; or, Homeopathy vs. Allopathy* (Virginia City: 1869). No copy of this pamphlet could be located.

Hines, H. K., *Illustrated History of The State Oregon* (Chicago: Lewis Pub. Co., 1893).

Holloway, Lisabeth M., *Medical Obituaries: American Physicians' Biographical Notices in Selected Medical Journals Before 1907* (N.Y.: Garland Pub., 1981).

Hulse, James W., *The Nevada Adventure: A History* (Reno: Univ. Nev. Press, 1972).

Hultkrantz, Åke, *The Religions of the American Indians* (Berkeley: Univ. Calif. Press, 1967).

Hultkrantz, Åke, *Shamanic Healing and Ritual Drama: Health and Medicine in Native North American Religious Traditions* (N.Y.: Crossroad Press, 1992).

Illustrated History of Baker, Grant, Malheur and Harney Counties with a Brief Outline of the Early History of the State of Oregon (Western Historical Pub. Co., 1902).

Investigation of the Charges Preferred by Wm. Thompson against Dr. S. Bishop (Carson City: SPO, 1887).

James, Edward T., ed., *Notable American Women, 1607-1950: A Biographical Dictionary* (Cambridge, Mass.: Belkanp Press, 1971).

Jones, J. Roy, *Memories, Men and Medicine: A History of Medicine in Sacramento, California* (Sacramento: Premier Pub., 1950).

Jones, Kathleen, *Asylums and After: A Revised History of the Mental Health Services: From the Early 18th Century to the 1990s* (London: Athlone Press, 1993).

Kelly, Howard Atwood, & Walter L., Burrage, *Dictionary of American Medical Biography*, (N.Y.: D. Appleton, 1928).

Kober, George Martin, *Reminiscences of George Martin Kober, M.D., LL.D.* (Menasha, WI: George Banta Pub. Co., 1930).

Larsell, Olaf, *The Doctor in Oregon: A Medical History* (Portland, Ore.: Binfords & Mort, 1947).

Leavitt, Judith Walzer, *Brought to Bed: Childbearing in America, 1750-1950* (N.Y.: Oxford Univ. Press, 1986).

Lewis, Marvin, *Martha and the Doctor: A Frontier Family in Central Nevada* (Reno: Univ. Nev. Press, 1977).

Lewis, Oscar, *Silver Kings: The Lives and Times of Mackay, Fair, Flood, and O'Brien, Lords of the Nevada Comstock Lode* (N.Y.: Alfred A. Knopf, 1947).

Lewis, Oscar, *The War and the Far West: 1861-1865* (Garden City, N.Y.: Doubleday & Co., 1961).

Lingenfelter, Richard E., *The Hardback Miners: A History of the Mining Labor Movement in the American West 1863-1893* (Berkeley: Univ. Calif. Press, 1974).

_____ and Karen Rix Gash, *The Newspapers of Nevada: A History and Bibliography, 1854-1979* (Reno: Univ. Nev. Press, 1984).

Lyman, George D., *The Saga of the Comstock Lode: Boom Days in Virginia City* (N.Y.: Charles Scribner's Sons, 1934).

McDonald, Douglas, Stanley W. Paher, ed., *The Legend of Julia Bulette and the Red light Ladies of Nevada* (Las Vegas: Nev. Pub., 1980).

Mack, Effie Mona, *History of Nevada* (Glendale, Calif.: Arthur H. Clark Co., 1935).

_____, *Mark Twain in Nevada* (N.Y.: Charles Scribner's Sons, 1947).

Marks, Paula Mitchell, *Precious Dust The American Gold Rush Era: 1848-1900* (N.Y.: Wm. Morrow & Co., 1994).

Michelson, Miriam, *The Wonderlode of Silver and Gold* (Boston: Stratford Co., 1934).

Norwood, William Frederick, *Medical Education in the United States Before the Civil War* (N.Y.: Arno Press & N.Y. Times, 1971).

Numbers, Ronald L., ed., *The Education of American Physicians* (Berkeley: Univ. Calif. Press, 1980).

Paden, Irene D., *The Wake of the Prairie Schooner* (N.Y.: Macmillan Co., 1943).

Paher, Stanley W., ed., *Nevada Towns and Tales* (Las Vegas: Nevada Pub., 1981-1982).

Patterson, Edna B., *Sagebrush Doctors and Health Conditions of Northeast Nevada from Aboriginal Times to 1972* (Springville: Utah Art City Pub. Co., 1972).

Paul, Rodman Wilson, *Mining Frontiers of the Far West 1848-1880* (N.Y.: Holt, Rinehart & Winston, 1963).

Perrone, Bobette, H. Henrietta Stockel, and Victoria Krueger, *Medicine Women, Curranderas, and Women Doctors* (Norman: Univ. Okla. Press, 1989).

Political History of Nevada, Ninth Edition, (Carson City: SPO, 1990).

Pulte, Joseph Hippolyt, Homeopathic Domestic Physician, Containing the Treatment of Diseases; Popular Explanations of Physiology, Hygiene, Hydropathy, Anatomy and Surgery, and an Abridged Materia Media (Cincinnati: Smith & Parks [etc.], 1850).

Ratay, Myra Sauer, *Boom Times in Old Washoe City, Nevada* (Sparks, Nev.: Western Print. & Pub. Co., 1984).

Read, Effie O., *White Pine Lang Syne: A True History of White Pine County, Nevada* (Denver: Big Mountain Press, 1965).

Read, Jay Marion and Mary E. Mathes, *History of the San Francisco Medical Society,* Vol. 1, 1850-1900, (San Francisco: James H. Barry, 1958).

Richards, Ralph T., *Of Medicine, Hospitals, and Doctors* (Salt Lake City: Univ. Utah Press, 1953).

Risse, Guenter B., Ronald L. Numbers and Judith Walzer Leavitt ed., *Medicine without Doctors: Home Health Care in American History* (N.Y.: Sci. Hist. Pub., 1977).

Rosenberg, Charles S., *Explaining Epidemics and Other Studies* (N.Y.: Cambridge Univ. Press, 1992).

Ross, Silas E., *Alphabetical Directory of Physicians and Surgeons of Record who have Practice Medicine in the Territory and State of Nevada From 1855 to March 1, 1957 with Short Biographical Sketch of Each.*

Rothstein, William G., *American Physicians in the Nineteenth Century: From Sects to Science* (Balto.: Johns Hopkins Univ. Press, 1972).

Roster of Regimental Surgeons and Assistant Surgeons in the U.S. Army Medical Department During the Civil War (Gaithersburg, Md.: Olde Soldier Books, Inc., 1989).

Scrugham, James G., ed., *Nevada, A Narrative of the Conquest of a Frontier Land*, I-III (Chicago: Amer. Hist. Soc. 1935).

Seagraves, Anne, *Women of the Sierra* (Lakeport, Calif.: Wesanne Enterprises, 1990).

Shryock, Richard H., *Medical Licensing in America, 1650-1965* (Balto: Johns Hopkins Univ. Press, 1967).

Simpson, Captain J. H., *Report of Explorations across the Great Basin of the Territory of Utah for a Direct Wagon-Route from Camp Floyd to Genoa, in Carson Valley, in 1859* (Reno: Univ. Nev. Press, 1983).

Sohn, Anton P., *A Saw, Pocket Instruments, and Two Ounces of Whiskey: Frontier Military Medicine in the Great Basin* (Spokane, Wash.: Authur H. Clark, 1997).

Sprague, William Forrest, *Women and the West A Short Social History* (Boston: Christopher Pub. House, 1940).

Starr, Paul, *The Social Transformation of American Medicine* (N.Y.: Basic Books, 1982).

Stewart, Robert E. & M. F., *Adolph Sutro* (Berkeley, Calif.: Howell & North Pub., 1962).

Stone, Eric, *Medicine Among the American Indians* (N.Y.: 1932).

Tinkham, George H., *A History of Stockton* (San Francisco: W. M. Hinton & Co., 1880).

Toll, David W., *Commitment to Caring: A History of Saint Mary's Hospital* (Reno: Nev. Academic Press, 1983).

Train, Percy, James R. Henrichs and W. Andrew Archer, *Medicinal Uses of Plants by Indian Tribes of Nevada* (Lawrence, Mass.: Quarterman Pub., Rev. 1957).

Tyson, James L., *Diary of a Physician in California* (Oakland, Calif.: Bilbooks, 1955).

Vogel, Virgil J., *American Indian Medicine* (Norman, Okla.: Univ. Okla. Press, 1970).

Walker, M. (Morris) R. (Rollins), *A life's Review and Notes on the Development of Medicine in Nevada From 1900 to 1944*, Second Revision (Reno: 1944).

_____, *Story of the Nevada State Society and Nevada Medicine* (Reno: 1937).

Wallnoser, Heinreich, and Anna von Rottauscher, *Chinese Folk Medicine and Acupuncture* (N.Y.: Bell Pub., 1965).

Wayman, John Hudson, ed. by E.W. Todd, *A Doctor on the California Trail* (Denver: Old West Pub. Co., 1971).

Winchell, Lilbourne Alsip, *History of Fresno County and the San Joaquin Valley* (Fresno: A.H. Cawston).

Wren, Thomas, *A History of the State of Nevada its Resources and People* (Chicago: Lewis Pub. Co., 1904).

Young, James Harvey, *The Toadstool Millionaires: A Social History of Patent Medicines in America before Federal Regulation* (Princeton, N.J.: Princeton Univ. Press, 1961).

Articles

Camargo, Carlos A., *"1492—The Medical Consequences,"* West. J. Med. 160, no. 6 (June 1994) pp. 545-553.

Cloud, Barbara, *"Images of Women in the Mining-Camp Press,"* Nev. Hist. Soc. Quart. 36, no. 3 (Fall 1993) pp. 194-207.

Courtwright, David, *"Opiate Addiction in the American West, 1850-1920"* J. West XXI, no. 3 (July 1982) pp. 23-31.

Driggs, Nevada W., *"How Come Nevada,"* Nev. Hist. Soc. Quart. XIV, no. 3 (Fall 1973) pp. 184-185.

Duffy, John *"Medicine in the West: an Historical Overview,"* J. West XXI, no. 3 (July 1982) pp. 5-14.

Fife, Austin E., *"Pioneer Mormon Remedies,"* Western Folklore 16, no. 3 (1957) pp. 153-162.

Hyatt, Robert M., *"The Restless Ghost of Doctor Montezuma,"* Frontier Times 38, no. 2, New Series no. 28 (Feb.-March 1964) pp. 28-30 and 72.

Herrick, H. S., *"Letters from a Nevada Doctor to his Daughter in Connecticut (1881-1891) Part I,"* Nev. Hist. Soc. Quart. 1, no. 1 (1957) pp. 15-31.

_____, *"Letters from a Nevada Doctor to his Daughter in Connecticut (1881-1891) Part II,"* Nev. Hist. Soc. Quart. 1, no. 2 (1957) pp. 81-97.

James, Susan, *"Queen of Tarts."* Nevada 44, no. 5 (1984) pp. 51-53.

Morrell, Joseph R., *"Medicine of the Pioneer Period in Utah,"* Utah Hist. Quart., XXIII (1955) pp. 127-144.

Oakberg, Helen Olmsted, and Annette Leighton Suverkrup, *"Dr. A.C. Olmsted Family,"* NE Nev. Hist. Soc. Quart. 94-1, pp. 28-35.

Pardini, Ronald S., et all, *"Inhibition of Mitochondrial Electron Transport by Nor-Dihydroguaiaretic Acid (NDGSA)"* Biochem. Pharm. 19 (1970) pp. 2695-2699.

Reifschneider, Olsa, *"Dr. Anderson in Wild and Wooly Carson City,"* Nev. Highways & Parks (Fall 1966).

Rocha, Guy, "*Regulating Public Health in Nevada: The Pioneering Efforts of Dr. Simeon Lemuel Lee*," Nev. Hist. Soc. Quart. XXIX (Fall 1986) pp. 201-209.

Rosenberg, Charles E., "*Medical Text and Social Context: Explaining William Buchan's Domestic Medicine*," Bull. Hist. Med. 57 (1983) pp. 22-42.

Russo, Elmer R., "Campaign Finance *Reform in the Silve Era: A Puzzle*" Nev. Hist. Soc. Quart. 38, no. 3 (1995) pp. 133-152.

Smith, Duane A., "*Comstock Miseries: Medicine and Mining in the 1860s*," Nev. Hist. Soc. Quart. 30, no. 1 (1993) pp. 1-12.

Smith, Phillip Dodd, Jr., "*The Sagebrush Soldiers: Nevada Volunteers in the Civil War*," Nev. Hist. Soc. Quart., 5, no. 3-4 (1987) pp. 3-87.

Thomas, Carin, et all, "Photoactivation of Hypericin Generates Singlet Oxygen in Mitochondria and Inhibits Succinoxidase," *Photochem. Photobio.* 55, no. 1 (1992) pp. 47-53.

_____, and Ronald S. Pardini, "*Oxygen Dependence of Hypericin-Induced Phototoxicity to EMT6 Mouse Mammary Carcinoma Cells*," Photochem. Photobio. 55, no. 6 (1992) pp. 831-837.

Newspapers (Years Published)

Carson Valley News (Genoa: Feb. 20, 1875- July 16, 1880).

Douglas County Banner (Genoa: Oct. 7, 1865-Dec. 23, 1865).

Elko Chronicle (Elko: Jan. 5, 1870-Dec. 4, 1870).

Elko Independent (Elko: June 19, 1869-Dec. 1914).

Genoa Journal (Genoa: Apr. 1-July 1880; Sept.-Dec. 22, 1880).

Genoa Weekly Courier (Genoa: July 23, 1880-June 2. 1899).

Humboldt Register (Winnemucca: Oct. 30, 1869-Dec. 1, 1876).

Nevada Staats Zeitung (Virginia City: Oct. 28, 1864-Dec. 1864)
   No known issues exist.

Nevada State Journal (Reno: Nov. 23, 1870-1902).

News (See Carson Valley News).

Pioche Weekly Record, 1872-1905.

Record-Courier (Gardnerville: April 8, 1904-1970+).

Reno Evening Gazette (March 28, 1876-1900+).

Silver State (Winnemucca: Sept. 10, 1874-July 11, 1925).

Territorial Enterprise (Nov. 3, 1860-Jan. 16, 1893; Dec. 3. 1893-
   May 30, 1916).

White Pine News (Ely, etc.: 1869-, Sept. 15, 1888-Dec. 30, 1923).

Unpublished Material, and Government Records

1860 U.S. Census (Utah Territory).

1870 U.S. Census (Nev.).

1875 Nev. Census.

1880 U.S. Census (Nev.).

1900 U.S. Census (Nev.).

Anderson, Charles Lewis, Papers, Univ. Calif. Bancroft Lib.

_____, Univ. Nev. Getchell Lib., Spec. Collect.

Baker, Sarah Catherine, "Basque American Folklore in Eastern
   Oregon," Berkeley, Calif., Univ. Calif., M.A. Thesis, 1972.

Barry, Patricia A., Interview by Anton P. Sohn, May 15, 1994.

"Beyond Gum San," A History of the Chinese in Nevada
   Exhibit, Nevada State Museum.

Blue, Helen M., "An Oral History on Albina Redner: A
   Shoshone Life," Reno, Univ. Nev., 1990.

Bross, Noeline Etchegoyhen, Interview by Anton P. Sohn,
   April, 21, 1997.

"Cooper Medical College Graduates," Palo Alto, Stanford Univ. Lane Med. Lib., Spec. Collect.

Corbusier, Fanny D., "Recollections of Her Life in the Army," Univ. Nev. Getchell Lib., Spec. Collect.

Cox, Leona M., "The Care Given to the Mentally Ill Prior to the Establishment of the Nevada State Hospital," Nursing Seminar Aug. 31, 1960, Reno, Univ. Nev. Lib., Spec. Collect.

Douglas Co. Recorder's ledgers, Minden, Nev.

Douglas Co. Tax List, Minden, Nev.

Duell, Paul D., "American Frontier Society and Chinese Medicine: The Dimension of an Interaction," Place and Practice: Regional Medicine, Health and Health Care in the Intermountain West, Conference in Reno, Nev., Oct. 22-23, 1993.

Dufurenna, Linda, "Marguerite Dufurenna Stephens Oral History," Winnemucca, 1994.

_____, "Pete Bengochea Oral History," Winnemucca, 1993.

Elko Co. Recorder's ledgers, Elko, Nev.

Esmeralda Co. Recorder's ledgers, Goldfield, Nev.

Esmeralda Co. Records (Lyon Co. Office).

Eureka Co. Recorder's ledgers, Eureka, Nev.

Grosh, Ethan, Letter to his father, Rev. A. B. Grosh, 1857.

Humboldt Co. Recorder's ledgers, Winnemucca, Nev.

Index to Journal of the Senate and Assembly of the Eighth Session of the Legislature of the State of Nevada (1875 Nevada Census) 2 and 3 (Carson City.: John Hill, State Printer, 1877).

Kober, George Martin, Manuscript, MS 315, Hist. Med. Div., Nat. Lib. Med., Bethesda, Md.

Lander Co. Recorder's ledgers, Austin, Nev.

LaVoy, Marian, Interview by Phyllis Cudek, Sept. 10, 1996.

Lee, Simeon L., Nat. Lib. Med., Box 3 MS C 142, Bethesda, Md.

Lincoln Co. Recorder's ledgers, Pioche,, Nev.

Luckey, Eugene, Interview by Anton P. Sohn, May 17, 1994.

Lyon Co. Recorder's ledgers, Yerington, Nev.

Mitchell Papers, Huntington Lib., Pasadena, Calif.

Nevada Board of Commissioners for Care of the Indigent Insane, Reno, Nevada, Investigation of Charges Against Dr. H. Bergstein Dec. 20, 1897, Univ. Nev. Lib., Spec. Collect.

Nevada Board of Medical Examiners records.

Nevada Centennial Committee for Early Day Families, Ormsby Co., 1964.

Nevada Centennial Committee for Early Day Families, White Pine Co., 1964.

Nevada State Museum Records, Carson City, Nev.

Nye Co. Recorder's ledgers, Tonopah, Nev.

Ogren, Carroll, "History of Washoe Medical Center," Reno.

Orsmby Co. Recorder's ledgers, Carson City, Nev.

Patterson, Edna B., "Florence Wines Sharp Oral History," Elko, Nev., 1958.

Saint Mary Louise Hosp. Adm. Records, Virginia City, Nev.

Sohn, Anton P., "Dr. Gerald J. Sylvain Oral History," Reno, Nev., Path. Depart., Univ. Nev. School Med., 1991.

Stewart Collect., Nev. Hist. Soc. Collect., Letter from doctors against antivivisectionists, U. S. Congress, Feb. 2, 1898.

Storey Co. Recorder's ledgers, Virginia City, Nev.

Thompson, Marie, Interview by Phyllis Cudek, Mar. 16, 1996.

Washoe Co. Med. Soc. and Nev. State Med. Assoc. Records.

Washoe Co. Recorder's ledgers, Reno, Nev.

White Pine Co. Recorder's ledgers, Ely, Nev.

Index

—M—

Mackay, John W., 27
Mackay, Marie Louise
Bryant, 27
Malpractice, 44
Manogue, Father
Patrick, 34
Manley, Dr. James F.,
29
Matthews, Dr.
Washington, 45
McBride, Dr. J. J., 101
McKnight, Dr., 80
McMeans, Dr.
Sheldon, 34
McMurtrey, Dr. A. T.,
101
Measles, 17, 37, 44, 73
Medicine Springs, 50
Meigs, Dr. John, 29
Midwife, 14, 84, 91
Minneer, Dr. William
S., 26
Moody, Eric, 179
Mormons, 70, 72, 84,
85, 97, 99

—N—

Neddenriep, Anna
Mueller Engel, 87
Neely, William, 27
Nevada Hospital for
Mental Disease, 30,
33

—O—

Ophthalmia, 75
Opium, 62, 63, 65, 94,
173, 174, 176
Osceola, Nev., 87
Owens Valley, Calif.,
40, 45, 80
Oxborrow, Mary
Leicht, 85

—P—

Panamint Mountains,
39
Pardini, Dr. Ronald, 54
Peterson, Mr., 26
Pinkerton, Dr.
Thomas H., 25, 26
Pleuritis, 75
Pneumonia, 50, 55, 72,
75, 87, 99